my
journey
through
the
spirit world

Ryuho Okawa

my

journey
through

the

spirit world

A TRUE ACCOUNT OF MY
EXPERIENCES OF THE HEREAFTER

Ryuho Okawa

IRH PRESS

BOOKS
IRH PRESS
New York

Library of Congress Cataloging-in-Publication Data

ISBN 13: 978-1-942125-41-9
ISBN 10: 1-942125-41-0

Printed in Canada

First Edition

Book Design: Karla Baker

Cover image© Liliya Linnik / Shutterstock.com

contents

Modern Developments in the Spirit World

CHAPTER FOUR

A Departure for the Afterworld

preface

In January 2005, the Japanese edition of my book *The Mystical Laws** received wide acclaim from my readers in Japan and became a national best-selling title. Many readers requested a sequel, prompting me to publish this book you hold in your hand to tell you what life is like in the spirit world—a fitting follow-up theme to the subject of life after death.

My Journey through the Spirit World may sound like a mystical title. But the spirit world is a place I visit just as naturally as you might step into your own backyard. In these pages, I have openly shared my personal experiences and what I think to be the truth about the other world. I am certain that this book will become many readers' guide to the radiant new afterworld of dazzling light. I'm certain that, by the time the world of the thirtieth century arrives, these truths will be accepted as common scientific knowledge.

---

* Ryuho Okawa, *The Mystical Laws* (Tokyo: IRH Press, 2015).

I will be delighted if this book also serves as a useful reference to those who wish to watch our animated film, *The Laws of Eternity*†, which I had the pleasure of producing.

Ryuho Okawa

Founder and CEO

Happy Science Group

---

† For more information about the movie, please contact the nearest Happy Science temple. The book that the movie was based on called, *The Nine Dimensions* (New York: IRH Press, 2012), by Ryuho Okawa, is also available in bookstores nationwide.

*life in the world
after death*

I

Modern People Have Lost an Understanding of Life after Death

The topic of life after death probably sounds provocative to many people living today, and a reasonable reaction to this topic may be to question the very existence of life after death. But this merely shows that the common knowledge that people in general share today does not accord with the spiritual Truths.

People today have gained much more detailed knowledge about various aspects of this world than people in the past had, but when it comes to the essential truths about the world that exists beyond this world, or the world after death, people in the past seem to have had a better understanding.

Many people think that belief in the afterworld is a primitive faith because they don't learn about it in schools or other educational institutions. As a result, they spend their lives in ignorance of it, which often causes a lot of confusion.

I don't think I can cover everything about the afterworld in a single book, so in this chapter, I would like to help you get a mental picture of what life after death is like.

Today, many people die in hospitals and spend their final days under the care of doctors. Medical scientists conduct studies about what happens up until we die but are at a complete loss to describe what happens after death. Traditionally, philosophy was the field of study that provided answers to questions about life after death. In fact, people learned about the other world in the time of Socrates and Plato. But contemporary philosophy has become a study of ancient Greek and German languages, the discipline's history, logic, and how to think. Unfortunately, philosophy no longer teaches truths about the other world.

Religion is the only field of study that deals with this subject, but different religions offer different teachings. Traditional religions are often obscure about the spirit world, and it is often difficult to decipher which of the new religions offer right teachings and which don't. Some religions provide accurate information about the afterworld, but others provide wrong information. This often creates confusion and makes people suspicious of religion altogether. In this context, I find it very encouraging that many intelligent, educated, and socially active people believe in Happy Science's teachings about the other world.

Souls Travel to the Spirit World during Sleep

The Silver Cord Links the Body to the Soul

What separates life from death? Your body contains a soul that is approximately the same shape as your physical body. Contrary to what you may believe, your soul doesn't remain inside your body all the time; when you sleep at night, your soul occasionally leaves your body.

While you sleep, you may sometimes have strange dreams that seem out of this world. For example, you may dream of flying or being chased by something frightening. Any dream that features full, natural colors and seems to be happening in a peculiar world may be an indication that your soul is visiting the spirit world.

What, then, is the difference between the souls of the dead and the souls of people who have temporarily left their bodies but are still alive? The souls of the living are linked to their bodies by the umbilical cord of the soul: the silver cord.

As its name suggests, this cord is silver in color, although because of the way it shines, it can also appear to have a slightly orange tint. This cord joins the body and soul at the top of the head. People throughout the ages and in all parts of the world have reported seeing this cord that connects the body and soul, and all these reports have been quite independent of one another.

Usually, your soul slips out of your body while you are asleep. When your soul, or your spiritual body, is near its physical counterpart, the silver cord is thicker than you might imagine. It resembles a thick rope with a diameter of four to five centimeters (1.5 to 2 inches). The inside looks like four to six strands of thick, wooly yarn twisted together. This is how thick the silver cord is when your soul remains close to your body. But as your soul moves away from your body, visits the spirit world, or travels beyond the stratosphere, it stretches until it becomes as thin as a spider's thread. Strange as it may seem, no matter how far it stretches, it will never get cut off and can extend to any length.

A great many people leave their bodies and visit the other world while they are asleep, and their silver cords remain attached. You may

What Is a Silver Cord?

The true moment of death:

The body and soul are connected by a silver cord. Once it gets cut off, the soul is no longer able to return to the physical body. So the true moment of death comes not when the brain stops functioning, but when the soul is no longer connected to the body by the silver cord. It generally takes about twenty-four hours after the heart stops beating for it to get severed.

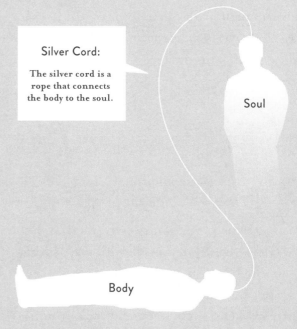

Silver Cord:

The silver cord is a rope that connects the body to the soul.

Soul

Body

People around the world have known about the silver cord since ancient times. Descriptions of it have been found in the Old Testament as well as in some books from the age of Socrates. Also, in Japan, the silver cord has traditionally been referred to as the "umbilical cord of the soul."

worry that your silver cord will get tangled, preventing your soul from returning to your body. In this world, cords such as threads and fishing lines easily get tangled. If it is not kept on a reel, a fishing line will soon become a mass of knots. Similarly, a dog left tied to a post will often wrap its leash around the post. But strangely, our silver cords never get tangled. Even if your silver cord crosses paths with other silver cords, it will just pass through them, stay untangled, and keep extending itself. This mysterious cord links your soul to your body.

☼

Cloudland: A Place We Visit during Sleep

As I just described, our souls often travel to the other world while we are asleep, with their silver cords attached. I can consciously observe the other world, but most people unconsciously visit the spirit world in their sleep and walk around unsteadily, with their eyes closed like sleepwalkers. A lot of them are in a half-asleep state and only open their eyes wide occasionally, when they come across something that particularly draws their notice. Once their souls return to this world, their conscious minds "translate" their experiences, so they remember them differently from what they saw in the spirit world.

Some travel to a specific area of the other world every night and take part in a particular activity on a regular basis. These people are engaged in a special job and interact with the inhabitants there while doing this job. But often they forget all about it once they wake up in the morning.

We may sometimes remember meeting with our deceased family members in our dreams even after we wake up. Recurring and continued dreams of meeting someone specific—for example, our father, mother, grandfather, grandmother, or brothers and sisters—mean that we really are meeting them in the other world.

If you have a specific hobby, you may visit people who share that interest and have a good time together. Some of the inhabitants of the other world spend all their time pursuing a hobby. For instance, those who enjoyed playing chess and were particularly good at it while they were alive usually continue to play after they return to the other world. These souls play against the living souls of chess players that have left their bodies during sleep. But the chess players forget all about it when they wake up the following morning and instead feel inspired to develop a new strategy or a good move. In this way, living souls often work with the souls in the other world to come up with new ideas and create something new. This may be what we do when we visit the other world.

We often call the world we visit during sleep "cloudland." Living souls can't venture very far into the spirit world and so often visit the area near the gateway to the Astral Realm of the fourth dimension. Those who are not in a good spiritual condition or are feeling mentally cornered may sometimes visit hell, but they are unlikely to travel to the depths of hell. They often visit and wander around shallow parts of hell that they can easily return from.

☼

There Is No Earthly Concept of Time or Space in the Other World

Our souls leave our physical bodies and travel to the other world while we are in what is medically referred to as REM sleep. REM stands for "rapid eye movement," because our eyes move rapidly during this stage of sleep. A complete sleep cycle is said to take about ninety minutes, and REM is one stage of this sleep cycle. It's during REM sleep that we have dreams, and this is also often when our souls travel to the spirit world. Our dreams usually last only about ten to twenty minutes, so our souls return to our physical bodies less than thirty minutes from the time they leave.

But as I have often said, earthly concepts of time and space do not exist in the other world. So even if you have visited the other world for only ten minutes of earthly time, you may feel as though you spent days there because you've experienced a variety of events that wouldn't fit into ten earthly minutes. You might feel as if you have returned from a long trip after meeting various types of people and gaining new experiences, but in fact it all happened in only about ten minutes of time in this world. This is because we can't measure time in the spirit world the same way we do in the physical world.

When we talk to souls in the spirit world, we always need to check time using the measurements of this world. In the other world, the same length of time can seem long or short depending on the amount of work or experience the soul has accumulated. So even though something may seem to have taken place over a long period of time, it may have taken only two or three days of earthly time. This shows how differently we experience time in the other world.

While we are still alive, we often visit the spirit world during sleep as a way of practicing for when we return to the other world after death. We spend about eight hours of every day asleep because if we don't practice while we are alive, we may find it difficult to move on to the next world after we die. Although most of us do this unawares, leaving the physical body in our sleep is nevertheless an essential practice.

3

What Happens to Those Who Refuse to Believe in the Afterworld?

What happens to those who stubbornly adhere to materialism and refuse to believe in the existence of the afterworld? What awaits those who deny the existence of the soul, God, Buddha, and anything beyond this world, those who firmly believe that religion is only a hoax and reject anything relating to religion, and those who think, "Everything ends with death, and it will be pitch black. So I will be numb after death"?

Even those who don't believe in the existence of the soul have souls, so when they die, their souls leave their bodies and travel to the other world. But because they are so adamant in their denial of the existence of the other world, they will not be able to recognize their surroundings, which will make it impossible for them to comprehend the fact that they are now in the spirit world.

These people become numb and motionless like waxworks, remaining almost unconscious. You may have heard of people who freeze themselves, saying, "I will come back to life a century later." Similarly, these souls wrap themselves in a sort of cocoon and remain completely oblivious to the world around them for decades, staying in the same condition they were in at the moment of their death. They remain unconscious and motionless until, after a long period of time, their firm denial of the existence of the spirit world wears away, like a huge sand dune that gradually crumbles as an army of ants carries away the sand grain by grain.

Dyed-in-the-wool materialists remain unconscious and motionless in the Unconsciousness Realm in hell* as if they are sleeping inside cocoons. We can find many people who do not believe in the afterlife lying in comas in a large cave-like place. What inhibits them from gaining consciousness is their denial of the existence of the other world and their belief that everything ends with death. They remain inactive

---

* The Unconsciousness Realm is a place where people who teach misguided philosophical or religious teachings and lead a lot of people astray go after death.

because their state of mind creates a cocoon that leaves them paralyzed.

During the decades that they remain unconscious, they gradually change their state of mind and start to vaguely feel that they are about to wake up from sleep. They realize that something is not right and begin to doubt their beliefs for the first time.

Eventually, they start to think, "Maybe I should try leaving the cavern," or they receive a visit from souls from other realms of the spirit world. It takes a lot of time, but these unconscious souls receive guidance from other inhabitants of the spirit world and gradually build up their experience of the afterlife. They are also sent to school in the spirit world to be reeducated. These souls are taught at school to learn the truth of the spirit world and to discard materialism and their belief that matter is everything.

4

Schools that Offer Spiritual Education Exist in Both Heaven and Hell

In the afterworld, schools exist in both heaven and hell. There is a big need for these schools because it's critical for new arrivals to the spirit world to receive spiritual education. Shortly after death, souls usually attend school either in the Astral Realm of heaven or in hell. In the school in hell, those who are on the way to becoming angels teach those who have held mistaken beliefs and returned to the shallow parts of hell but who will be able to return to heaven after receiving a thorough education about spiritual truths.

It takes patience to teach those who didn't believe in the existence of the spirit world when they were alive and had to spend time in hell as a result of their disbelief. Angels-to-be teach these people everything they need to know step by step until they attain a state of mind that will enable them to enter heaven. Active and devoted members of Happy Science will most likely become these angels-to-be when they return to the other world; this is the type of work they will engage in.

Even those who say they don't have faith or believe in any particular religion often do hold religious beliefs on a subconscious level. When asked straightforwardly in a survey for a newspaper or magazine whether they believe in any specific religion, usually only about 20 to 30 percent of Japanese respondents say they do. But this does not necessarily mean that the other respondents don't have faith.

Many people who say they don't believe in religion do have faith; it's just that they don't realize they do. For example, they pray for the repose of the souls of their deceased family members. They visit their family members' graves to tell their late grandparents that their grandson is doing well or that their granddaughter has just started primary school. In Japan, many of these people also visit a shrine or temple at the beginning of the new year to pray and make an offering.

Most of them simply do not have enough knowledge about the soul or the other world because these things are not taught in school, but they can still feel the existence of these things, albeit faintly. These people will not go to hell immediately following their deaths. Instead, they temporarily return to the Astral Realm, which is in the upper part of the Posthumous World of the fourth dimension that belongs to heaven. There, they attend a school and take classes taught by the angels-to-be.

Souls that are sent to school in the spirit world feel as though they have taken a one- or two-year course, but not much earthly time has passed; it is generally about a week to ten days or sometimes about one or two months. By the time they complete the course, they feel as if they have finished three years of high school, but they may find that only forty-nine earth days have passed since their death.

After they receive their education in the school of the spirit world and understand the laws that govern the other world, their friends or family members come to take them to the place where they will carry out the next stage of their spiritual training.

The Dimensional Structure
of the Other World

Ninth Dimension – The Cosmic Realm:
The realm of the saviors

Eighth Dimension – The Realm of Tathagatas:
The realm of spirits who were central figures in shaping
the history of particular eras

Seventh Dimension – The Realm of Bodhisattvas:
The realm of spirits whose main focus is on helping others

Sixth Dimension – The Realm of Light:
The realm of specialists and divine spirits

Fifth Dimension – The Realm of Goodness:
The realm of good-hearted spirits

**Fourth Dimension –
The Posthumous Realm:**
The realm where people go
immediately after death

Hell

Hell is much smaller
than Heaven; it exists
in the lower part of the
Posthumous Realm.

**Third Dimension
– Earthly Realm**

life in the world after death

5

Spirits Go through Shocking Experiences in Hell

What Happens to Those Who Fall Deep into Hell?

The souls who attend school in the spirit world are those whose mindsets and behaviors as human beings were acceptable. Those who fall straight to a deep part of hell have not yet reached a level to receive education at the school in the spirit world. They are sent straight to hell to go through all kinds of experiences. It would simply be impossible to educate all of them together in the same school, so they are forced to go through awful experiences as individuals until they can see their faults for themselves. The kinds of experiences that they have to go through vary depending on each soul. They are sent to the realms that manifest the tendencies of their minds or the thoughts they hold onto most strongly. Their experiences there can be very shocking and intense.

※

Souls Can't Find Salvation
Until They Are Ready to Repent

Let's say a murderer dies and falls to hell without repenting his crime. He will likely go to a realm filled with murderers. There he will find other souls who are more vicious and aggressive than he is, so he will probably experience being murdered repeatedly. He may be able to defeat souls that are weaker than him, but he will be killed when he faces stronger souls. He will go through the experiences of killing and being killed repeatedly, day after day, until he realizes how awful it is to murder someone.

Although I've used the word *kill*, these souls cannot technically kill one another because they no longer have physical bodies. But they can feel the pain of being killed, because they still have the spiritual nerves that transmit pain to their souls.

Those who killed others or inflicted injury

while they were alive—or tried to and were killed or injured in return—inflicted suffering on others. Those who did not endure such sufferings during their lifetimes in this world do not know how painful it feels to be killed or injured. But those who did kill or harm others when they were alive become very susceptible to pain once they return to the other world.

When souls kill in the spirit world, they see blood gushing out of the person, so they think, "He is dead." But after a short while, the person they thought they'd killed rises to his feet. When they are defeated and are killed by others, they think they are dead, but before long, they find themselves able to rise again. They start killing one another all over again, engaging in endless battles. It's like when the mafias of this world are engaged in bitter strife.

These souls fight mercilessly but gradually become sickened by the endless cycle of killing and begin to think, "I've had enough of this already." Every time they think they have killed their enemy and triumphed, the enemy comes back to life and kills them in turn. After they go through these experiences repeatedly for some time, most of them come to feel that they've had enough. They say to themselves, "Come to think of it, this was exactly the kind of life I had when I was alive" and realize that their lives were filled with nothing but fear, hatred, and destruction. And they gradually become sickened by this lifestyle. This state of mind often leads them to awaken to aspirations of enlightenment or a desire to achieve a state of spiritual awareness.

They can only leave this realm when they become determined to distance themselves from this kind of lifestyle. Right about when they start to think, "I want to cut my ties with this world," help arrives: someone who has a spiritual connection to them comes down from heaven to offer assistance.

It really is a daunting task to go down to such an atrocious place to save the souls there. You can imagine how difficult it would be if you had to rescue someone from an organized-crime syndicate. Even an undercover agent wouldn't be willing to take on that task alone, because it would mean putting his life at risk. It indeed is a difficult task to save souls from the underworld.

For help to come, those who have fallen to such a world first need to repent and hold a wish to leave. These thoughts lessen their power in that realm: by becoming a "good person," they become weak in a world of violence. Those who have become sickened by their way of life become vulnerable to attacks by those who want to aggressively harm them.

When this happens to someone, other souls notice it and start beating and battering him, saying, "This guy used to be really strong, but he has gotten so much weaker." The ones who want to leave have to bear this hardship; they need to endure until others lose interest and get tired of bullying such weak souls. They only receive a helping hand after others have abandoned them.

6

This World and the Other World Are Closely Linked to Each Other

Iraqi Soldiers Continue to Fight in the Afterworld

When many people die unexpectedly in a war or disaster, most of them haven't had the chance to prepare themselves for death, so they initially find themselves in a realm of hostility of their own making, such as the Hell of Agonizing Cries or the Hell of Strife (Ashura Realm).

For instance, according to a high-end estimate, more than a hundred thousand Iraqi soldiers died in the first Gulf War when coalition forces led by the United States fought the Iraqi forces that had invaded Kuwait. U.S. leaders felt that they could not sit back and watch as Iraq invaded its peaceful neighbor, so they formed a military alliance to expel the Iraqi troops from Kuwait.

When such a large number of people die within a short period of time, a realm of hell appears in either the Ashura Realm or a deeper part of hell, such as the Hell of Agonizing Cries. A realm like this appeared during the Gulf War, and the Iraqi soldiers who died in that war went to that realm and continued to fight the war.

According to Islam, when men die fighting for the sake of Allah, they return straight to heaven, where they are surrounded by beautiful women who offer them alcohol and an abundance of delicacies. But when these Iraqi soldiers look around, they don't see any of these things, so they think, "Oh, we are still alive." These souls continue to fight in a dark mist, ignorant of the fact that they are dead.

The number of casualties among U.S. forces is said to be about 150, but this is too few souls to create a realm of hell. For a group this size, each soul receives one-to-one attention and is led to a place that corresponds to the level of their awareness as individuals, so there is no specific realm that they all return to. This means that no matter how hard the Iraqi soldiers search for their enemy in the other world, they won't be able to find them. The only souls they will meet in the afterworld will be their allies, not their enemies.

In the ground battle in the desert, the Iraqis used obsolete Soviet tanks while the Americans had the latest armored vehicles. It was initially thought that the two forces had approximately the same fighting capabilities, but once the battle began, it became obvious that the Soviet tanks were much weaker than had been thought, and the American forces won a resounding victory. The Iraqi tank regiments were virtually wiped out, while the Americans suffered practically no losses.

Such overwhelmingly superior military strength of one party over the other was almost unheard of, but the technological gap between the Iraqi forces and the American forces made it happen. During the war, Americans used depleted uranium shells, which are extremely dense and heavy. One single shell was all they needed to penetrate the armor of an Iraqi tank and destroy the whole tank. On the other hand, the shells that the Iraqis used could not penetrate the armor of the American tanks; they could damage the outside of the tanks but not the inside. Moreover, the Iraqis' old Soviet tanks had to be operated manually; when the

enemy tanks moved, they had to rotate the tur-
ret to track them. But the Americans' state-of-
the-art tanks had turrets that could automati-
cally track their targets, even if they moved. The
result of these differences in technology was the
defeat and almost complete destruction of the
Iraqi tank units.

☼

In the Spirit World, Weapons Are Only Effective against Enemies Who Recognize Them

You may believe that only our souls, spirits,
and spiritual bodies travel to the other world
after death, but this is not true: objects can also
travel to the other world. When material objects
with certain functions or shapes cease to exist in
this world, they can appear in the spirit world.

When the Iraqi tank brigade was destroyed on
Earth, the Iraqi tanks appeared in the Ashura
Realm where the Iraqi soldiers went when they
died. These tanks can function in the other world,
but there is no enemy that they can fight against,
because they can't find a single American tank in
their world. While the Iraqis are searching for
their enemy, they may encounter warriors from

ancient times that inhabit the Ashura Realm. When this happens, an interesting scene may take place.

The other world is a world of the mind, so if you believe that something exists, it manifests itself. So what happens when the Iraqi soldiers encounter the ancient warriors armored with bows and arrows and turn their cannons on them? The Iraqi tanks fire on the ancient warriors, but to the surprise of the Iraqi army, the shells don't explode. They don't understand why, and the Iraqis fire a second salvo only to find that the same thing happens again: the shells hit the enemy but don't explode. No matter how many shells they fire, not one of them explodes.

The reason for this is that the ancient warriors don't know what tanks or cannon shells are. They watch them, wondering, "What are those round flying balls coming out of a box-like moving object?" These warriors aren't frightened by the shells at all, because they don't know what they are supposed to do to them. In the spirit world, the weapons are powerless unless the other party recognizes what they are, so these artillery shells are ineffective against warriors who have no idea what they are.

If we want to fight the ancient warriors in the spirit world, we would be better off throwing stones at them. If we throw stones or fight with bows and arrows or spears, the ancient warriors will understand immediately what they are. But they won't feel anything and won't even recognize that they are under attack when they see tanks firing their cannons at them.

To their eyes, an airplane simply looks like a giant bird in the sky, so when they see an airplane dropping a bomb on them, they see the bomb as just a large bird dropping. The dropped bomb doesn't explode, because they think it's simply a bird dropping, and they suffer no damage from it.

In the spirit world, when we fight against ancient warriors, modern weapons are completely ineffective, so we need to fight them in a way they can comprehend, which means fighting with our fists or blades. These are effective because they are the methods they use in fighting battles; they recognize that they'll suffer cuts and pain if they fight in this way. But fighting against them using weapons they don't recognize is futile.

If the Iraqis were "lucky" enough to come across German soldiers who died in one of the world wars, they would be able to use tank warfare. The German soldiers know what tanks are, so if the Iraqis fired shells from their "modern" Soviet tanks, the Germans would fight back with their outdated German tanks. Because the German troops would recognize the Iraqis' weapons, they would get frightened, and when the shells exploded, they would cry out in fear and get blown apart by the bomb's blast.

When two opponents who both understand modern weaponry confront each other, both suffer damage. But if one party cannot recognize the other party's weapons, no harm can be done. We can find virtually all kinds of earthly weapons in the spirit world, but they are ineffective against those who do not know their potential.

Everyone in the modern world is aware of the destructive power of atomic bombs, so if an atomic bomb were dropped on modern people in the afterworld, they would recognize it and collapse, thinking, "I was killed by the bomb." But if it were dropped on people who had lived in the distant past, it would be harmless. They don't know what an atomic bomb is, so there is no way that they could comprehend its destructive capability.

All kinds of weapons exist in hell, from tanks

to knives. But these weapons can threaten us only if we recognize them. A machine gun will do us no harm if we don't know what it can do. Believe it or not, this is the reality in the afterworld.

☼

Demolished Buildings Appear in the Afterworld

Buildings from this world can also appear in the world after death. If a several-decades-old building is torn down, it can appear in the other world exactly as it was before its demolition. For instance, each museum in this world has unique spiritual vibrations that are created by the sum of various elements, including the intentions of the person who built it, the mindset of the curator, and the artworks displayed there—which include both ones that have the vibrations of heaven and ones with vibrations of hell.

When a museum with heavenly vibrations gets old and is torn down and replaced by a new building, it appears in a realm of heaven that corresponds to its overall spiritual vibrations. It looks exactly as it did on Earth, and those who are qualified to visit the museum in heaven will start going there.

Paintings in this museum that had heavenly vibrations appear in the museum in heaven exactly as they did on Earth. These are ethereal counterparts of the paintings that come into existence in the spirit world. Paintings that had negative vibrations, on the other hand, even if they were displayed at the same museum, disappear from the museum in heaven.

By contrast, a museum that was operated by an ill-hearted curator who collected and displayed artworks with negative vibrations appear in hell when the museum is demolished. If you were to visit a museum in hell, you would find many deformed versions of the paintings that the museum had displayed in this world. The paintings there look uglier, more terrifying, and grotesque. But these paintings don't look horrendous at all to those who enjoyed this kind of art while they were alive. In fact, they may find them to their liking.

Paintings that are considered masterpieces in this world do not all have the same spiritual vibrations. When they return to the spirit world, they will appear in the places that are appropriate to their spiritual level.

I once visited a museum in France that had many exhibits of paintings by Van Gogh, and I remember feeling very dizzy while I was there. It felt okay to see just one of his paintings, but when I found myself surrounded by them, I felt as if I had entered into a bizarre world, and my head began to spin. There was something abnormal about Van Gogh's works.

I believe that many people like Edvard Munch's paintings, but his most famous work, *The Scream*, has a creepy aura and the negative vibrations of hell. Although a painting may be considered a masterpiece in this world, its destination in the other world will depend on its spiritual vibrations, which are influenced by factors such as the artist's intentions and viewers' reactions.

A similar thing happens to libraries. When a library is demolished, its ethereal entity appears in the spirit world. The library appears in heaven if the majority of its collection is books with heavenly vibrations and it's run by a good-hearted director. The inhabitants of heaven will be able to study in it or use its books for their research.

Interestingly, most of the newly published books in this world also appear in the spirit world. They are stored in the libraries that are appropriate for the vibrations of each book. Some of these books go to hell. The libraries in hell contain many books that are too hideous for heavenly spirits to think of, such as pornographic books and books about how to kill people and how to commit suicide. People are free to publish what they like, but when they publish books that invite evil or lead people to commit crimes, their books end up in the libraries of hell.

Earlier, I mentioned the realm of hell that murderers end up in. Some of these spirits are very intelligent. Intelligence does not determine our destination in the other world; some of them go to heaven, and others fall to hell.

White-collar criminals study in the libraries of hell to search for more efficient ways of killing people. They may read about how the guillotine was used in the old days and think, "Wow. This is amazing. I wonder if I can reproduce it or create a newer, more efficient model." The libraries of hell have huge collections of books on how to kill people. Intelligent criminals there study to improve their intellectual ability so that they can commit more brutal acts. Many clever, intelligent people commit heinous crimes in this world. When members of organized groups return to the other world, they continue to polish their intelligence in the libraries of hell.

Among the schools in the afterworld are ones that were demolished in this world. When an old, wooden school building gets torn down, for example, its ethereal entity appears in the other world. This is because a lot of people studied there for years and still remember the school building. These school buildings are used both in realms of hell and in the Astral Realm in heaven. When souls return to the other world, they see these school buildings and recall memories of their school days.

On September 11, 2001, the twin towers of the World Trade Center in New York were completely destroyed. When an entire building collapses like that, it will generally appear in the spirit world. But when I consider the intention behind the destruction of the World Trade Center, how it was destroyed, and the misery and tragedy its destruction has caused in the lives of several thousand people, I think it's unlikely that it appeared in heaven. It probably appeared in a realm of hell, and pandemonium probably continues to reign there.

I believe that the World Trade Center will

eventually move up to heaven, when the souls of the thousands of victims who lost their lives in the attack find salvation and return to heaven. But at the time of writing this, it has only been three years since the attack, so I think it is still a site of carnage where the souls of the deceased experience the same scenes over and over as they repeatedly run around in search of a place to flee the flames or jump out of windows. I believe that this situation will probably continue for some time until these souls are saved. These are some examples that show how closely linked events in this world are to events in the other world.

Inventions in this world also appear in the other world when the inhabitants there acknowledge them. For instance, there are trains in the afterworld. Because a large number of people take trains to go to work and school everyday, they would find it inconvenient to get around without them. Trains appear to those who think they need them. But trains only exist in the lower realms where the spirits still maintain earthly lifestyles; they do not exist in the higher dimensions of heaven.

Butcher Shops in the Spirit World
Need No Stock

Those who reside in the realms of the spirit world that are relatively close to this physical world still wish to maintain a lifestyle like the one they had when they were alive. So some of them continue to eat food. But they only feel like they're eating, because no matter how much they believe they have eaten, there is no real food there. It feels as though the food they consume disappears like melting snow before reaching their stomachs. This is their eating experience in the spirit world. But they continue this habit because they want to experience the sensation of eating.

Shops and stores exist in the other world because those who owned shops in this world often wish to continue their businesses in the afterworld. In the lower reaches of the spirit world, the inhabitants often stay in the same occupations they had in the physical world, so we can find individual stores that sell meat, fish, or vegetables.

A big difference between shops in this world and the ones in the other world is that the owners have no need to restock, because the goods always come back to where they were. Let's say someone goes to the butcher shop thinking, "I want to make a meat dish for dinner." She buys a broiler, brings it home, cooks it, and eats it, but the next time she passes by the shop, she will see the exact piece of meat she purchased back in the store. In addition, when she purchases the meat, she will pay for it, but it's not like she's paying with real money; she only feels like she has paid for it.

The customer who bought the broiler feels like she has savored a delicious meal, but she doesn't feel like it is in her stomach. And before she knows it, the meat has returned to the shop and is on display in the shop window. The same thing happens if she buys vegetables; the vegetables that she buys, cooks, and eats will return to the vegetable shop. The inhabitants of the spirit world's lower reaches go through these same routines over and over. These people are among the many who have only reached a rudimentary level of awareness even after returning to the spirit world.

7

Inhabitants of the Spirit World Use Mental Power to Create and Transform Objects

The Schools in the Other World Teach Spirits to Create Objects at Will

The area of the spirit world that I've just described is relatively close to the physical world. In a higher area, above that one, the inhabitants understand that what they think of will appear, so they start to create things using the power of their will.

Spirits residing there often receive training in creation. For instance, they attend study sessions where they learn how to make a blooming tulip appear. They conduct experiments to prove that the spirit world is a world of thoughts and to practice manifesting their thoughts. A teacher assembles students, saying, "I am going to demonstrate how to produce things using my willpower, so please watch carefully," and instantaneously produces a single red tulip out of nowhere. The teacher then tells the students to follow her example. The students try, but the tulips they produce are often twisted, wilted, or of a different color. Creating something by will is quite difficult; it only appears when we can picture what we want to produce vividly, down to the last detail.

Students usually begin their training by producing small items. As they progress, they try to create more complicated objects, such as dogs. The teacher concentrates her will for a moment, and a dog appears. It looks exactly like a real dog, and it starts moving around, wagging its tail, and licking people. It seems like magic to the students, who say to each other, "Wow. That's so impressive. Our teacher is really amazing."

When the students try to imitate their teacher, however, they find themselves unable to create dogs and instead end up creating all kinds of incomplete, weird creatures. Someone suggests, "Why don't we try working together in groups of about ten? Maybe we can achieve better results if we join forces." Together they focus their will on the animal they wish to create, and gradually they begin to produce pigeons, dogs, and cats.

When a large number of people bring their

thoughts together to create something in the other world, their creation will continue to exist for some time. The collective thoughts of the spirit world's inhabitants reconstruct spiritual phenomena and give rise to astral bodies that didn't exist before.

Dogs and cats that are willed into existence stay alive for a while, and the inhabitants of the spirit world can keep them as pets. But when everyone forgets about them, they disappear. Among the living creatures we find in the other world are ones that came back after their physical lives ended, but we can also find many creatures that were created there.

Monsters Are Created in Hell

As you can probably imagine from the fact that animals can be created, in hell, it is also possible to create frightening creatures such as monsters. Some of the monsters in hell were originally human beings who transformed into monsters when they went to hell. These creatures are real existences that have spiritual bodies, but there are others that were created in hell. These creatures manifest when evil thoughts from this world and from hell come together and take shape as giant monsters or demons that do evil. These giant monsters exist in the world of murderers.

There are a wide variety of monsters in hell, including man-eaters. Some of these monsters are original life forms, but many others were produced in the other world. The ones that were created in the spirit world undergo a sudden transformation when the evil energy or thoughts that created them are removed. In many cases, different entities reside inside these monsters, and resume their original form when the evil is removed. Evil creatures do exist in hell, but when evil spirits in hell cannot capture the monsters they want, they often create them.

✷

Powerful Demons Can Turn Their Minions into Dogs

Those with extremely strong willpower, such as demons with many underlings, can even turn other inhabitants of hell into animals. For instance, let's say a demon gets his minions together to raid, loot, and seize a neighboring village and return with several dozen villagers as slaves who need to be locked in a hut and guarded. The most effective way to guard these captives is to keep them too terrorized to escape, and vicious dogs are often useful for that purpose.

But dogs in general do not commit acts of evil, so they are rarely found in hell. So the demon has no option but to create vicious guard dogs himself. He typically starts by looking around for a minion that looks like a dog. Once he finds someone, he focuses his will on his minion and turns him into a dog.

Of course, the minion will resist being turned into a dog, but the demon will tell him, "You are a guard. If you don't look like a vicious dog, you won't be able to terrify our captives. I need you to roar at them and scare them to death so they won't even think about escaping." The unwilling minion is forced to become a guard dog.

The other world is a world of thought, so those with the strongest willpower can transform others. With the power of their will alone, these demons can create vicious dogs with large fangs that can bite to death anybody who tries to escape.

These are some of the things that are happening in the other world. Thoughts become reality. And in the world of hell, when one will comes into conflict with another, the more powerful will wins, and the weaker one has to surrender and obey the winner.

When war breaks out in hell, there are never enough horses to go around, because, like dogs, horses are basically good-natured creatures, and very few of them end up in hell. So, powerful demons turn their minions into horses to engage in battle.

Many substances in hell can be transformed into different things. Even inanimate objects and spirits of plants and trees can be morphed into different entities when they come under the control of a spirit with strong mental power.

All this may sound extremely strange, but you may be able to imagine what it's like if you think of a world where only thoughts exist. If you hold an image in your mind strongly enough, it will manifest. In the spirit world, your strong wishes will come true.

Broken Goods Are Repeatedly Restored

The spirit world is a place where like-minded souls congregate. There is a world of those who enjoy eating but never become full, no matter how much food they consume. Vicious murderers reside in a world where the killing never ends, because no matter how many times they kill the same person, he will come back to life every time. Even if they cut someone's head off, a new head will grow back after a while. And if they are killed in turn, they will rise to their feet again. This situation eventually becomes unbearable.

As I have described, buildings from this world appear in the afterworld when they are demolished. In hell, vicious murderers walk around destroying the buildings that have appeared there. But as soon as they walk past buildings they've destroyed, they reappear as if nothing had happened. No matter how many times these buildings are destroyed, they are always restored to their original condition. They disappear when spirits with destructive thoughts are nearby but return as soon as those spirits move away.

In the same way, destroyed and broken objects are endlessly restored to their original condition. You may be able to better understand how the spirit world works if you think of it as a place that continues to exist as long as people keep thinking the thoughts that create the world.

The spirit world is home to spirits who go through the cycle of reincarnation between this world and the other world, as well as spirits that stay in the spirit world permanently and never come into the physical world, such as nature spirits. There are also other types of spiritual entities that belong to neither group, many of which have been created by the spirits. Something that a large number of people feel a need for, or something whose existence a large number of people believes in, appears in the spirit world as a manifestation of the common will of many people.

Mythical creatures such as dragons no longer exist in this world, but they do exist in the spirit world. Dragon-gods that defend shrines and temples in heaven are not necessarily dragon spirits, however. Although they are not the same as the minions that are turned into dogs in hell, in some cases the guardian god of a temple or a shrine may take on the shape of a dragon to guard it and intimidate any intruders. We see these guardian dragons in heaven, and we see venomous dragons in hell. Many of these transformed spirits appear when they have become objects of worship for many people.

8

Spirits in Hell Can Haunt People in this World

The Afterlife Is the Real World—
the Physical World Is Only a Temporary Abode

The other world may seem unreal, like a place out of a dream, but in fact it is the *real* world. It is extremely important that we recognize the truth that the afterlife is the real world and this physical world is only a temporary abode, a dreamlike place. Acknowledging this will allow us to become a member of the spirit world.

We need to awaken to the truth that the other world is no dream, even though it may seem that way. It is an eternal world, a world that will last forever. This world, on the other hand, is a transient and impermanent place, although it seems very real to us. This is why Buddhism teaches people to abandon all attachments to the physical world.

I am sure that this world appears real to everyone reading this book. You probably think that everything in this world actually exists, and you may even feel that that this world is all there is. But if that's what you think, you need to shift your perspective 180 degrees.

Nothing in this world lasts forever. In contrast, beings in the other world can continue to exist indefinitely and can freely transform themselves in any way they want. The other world is truly a mysterious place of eternal existence and transfiguration.

☼

Spirits in Hell See Trash as Treasure

The ways spirits see things in the other world vary greatly depending on their spiritual states. For example, those who have strong attachments to jewelry, money, lavish attire, or any other valuable goods in this world will try to obtain them in the other world unless they cast aside these attachments before they return there.

If these people end up in hell, they may break into luxurious houses and steal diamond rings, necklaces, gold, or anything valuable they can find. They would put on the rings, necklaces, and beautiful clothes that they stole, saying, "Yay! Look at all the jewelry I got! It all looks so beautiful!" To these spirits, the items they steal look like treasures, but to spirits in heaven, the thieving spirits appear delighted to be wearing jewels made of charcoal and clothing made of trash. These heavenly spirits wonder, "Why in the world do they take delight in wearing trash?" But what looks like trash in the eyes of the heavenly spirits appears as treasure to the inhabitants of hell. This truly is a wonder of the spirit world.

The spirits in hell have never seen the light of heaven or the stunning jewelry that exists there. Even if they tried to see these things, they would be too dazzling for the spirits in hell to even tell what they are. The inhabitants of hell see trash as jewels, so they adorn themselves with trash, believing that it's jewels. (Jewels and precious metals do exist in heaven, too. They simply appear different depending on the motives and purposes of the people looking at them.) What the spirits of hell are doing is utter silliness, but they continue to act that way until they realize the vanity of it.

Some people cling to the love relationships they had in this world. When they return to the other world, they will need to let go of these attachments so they can concentrate on their training there. To help these people, at the entrance to heaven, men and women are often divided into separate groups to start their training.

At the beginning of their training in heaven, men and women are separately given lectures on the spirit world to purify their souls. They need to be educated this way until they lose their physical attachments to the opposite sex. After a certain period of time, men and women are free to date each other and live together. It is just that they need to receive some of their training separately until they can cast away their worldly desires.

In hell, men and women continue to have sexual relationships like the ones they had when they were alive. But like the murderers who find themselves unable to kill others in hell, these men and women can never satisfy their sexual desires, because they no longer have physical bodies. These spirits cannot physically kill or embrace each other because they have become mere ghosts.

Total Possession Occurs When the
Soul Becomes Unable to Control Its Own Body

When the inhabitants of hell realize that, without their corporeal bodies, they can't take any tangible action and they can't really destroy anything, no matter how much they try, they feel stumped about what to do. Other, more experienced spirits come to them, saying, "Let me tell you a secret. All you have to do is possess a person in the physical world, and you will be able to experience whatever that person experiences." In this way, spirits in hell discover a way to get out of the situation they've been put in.

Spirits who couldn't satisfy their appetites no matter how much they ate can visit a restaurant or bar and find people who are eating and drinking. They simply have to find someone whose vibrations are similar to their own to possess that person's body, and then can experience the sensations of eating and drinking. They can't experience these sensations as spiritual beings, but once they enter a physical body by possessing a person in this world, they enjoy the meal and feel the texture of the food on their tongues. They get addicted to the experience of feeling these physical sensations.

What do you think happens to the soul of a person who has been possessed by a spirit from hell? When someone is completely possessed by another spirit, his soul is forced out of his body, although the silver cord still connects his soul to his body. The soul that has been pushed out hovers around the body in a dither, saying, "Oh no, my body has been hijacked. What should I do? What should I do?"

The overbearing spirit that has taken over the body looks gruesome. It has a huge mouth that extends to its ears, horns grow out of its head, and its eyes are aflame with desire. The person's soul had to leave its body to flee from such a frightening spirit. And when the soul flees the body, the intruder slips in to eat, drink, and visit fleshpots, indulging in all the physical pleasures that he wasn't able to indulge in when he was alive.

When spirits possess the living, they can temporarily gain control of those people's physical bodies and feel as if they have been reborn. These spirits cannot be reborn directly from hell. They can only experience life in this world by spiritually possessing someone who is alive.

But they eventually have to leave the bodies they've seized when the possessed come back to their senses.

Drinking alcohol often makes us lose our ability to think rationally and so makes it easier for an evil spirit to possess us, especially when we engage in morally wrong activities in the company of many accomplices. But the invading spirits can't stay in the physical bodies for long, and they are eventually forced to leave. But when an evil spirit possesses the same person every day, the spirit eventually starts to occupy the body continuously and gains complete control over it. When this happens, the possessed person loses control of his own body almost completely.

You may have heard of people who have no memory of committing the crimes they are accused of. These people insist, "I was unconscious at the time of the crime. I had no intention of doing that, and I have no idea how it happened. I don't remember anything." In many cases, what they are saying is true; it all happened while they were unconscious, and they don't remember a thing.

This is because the soul was forced out of the body and another spirit took over. It is actually the evil spirit that possessed them that did all the bad things, such as committing murder, robbery, and shoplifting. The souls of the possessed come back to their bodies only after the fact, when the evil spirits have left.

The next thing these people know, they're standing trial for crimes they don't remember at all. When asked if they committed the crimes they're accused of, they can only answer, "I don't remember doing any of it." But contrary to their memory, witnesses identify them and testify, "This person committed the murders and robberies at such and such a time on the night of such and such a day." The accused protest, "I have no memory of doing any of it. I didn't do it," but to no avail.

What really happened to these people is an evil spirit took control of their bodies, committed crimes, and then left the scene, gloating over their villainy. These evil spirits couldn't care less what happens to the people they possess— whether they're sentenced to life in prison or even to death—once they leave their bodies. But when these people are charged with the spirits' crimes, they refuse to accept it and struggle to get away from their bitter fate.

☀

Spirits that Repeatedly Commit Evil Are Banished to the Nethermost Hell

Spirits that possess living people repeatedly to commit acts of evil build up a record in hell of their sins. They may be grateful to whichever spirit told them about the trick of possessing people in the physical world. But if they continue to possess people to commit crimes one after another, killing people, destroying their lives, or leading them to fall into a debt trap, they will no longer be able to remain in that realm of hell and will find themselves suddenly dropping down to a lower level.

This won't discourage them from possessing living people, and they'll keep repeating evil acts and falling deeper and deeper into hell. The more powerful they become and the higher they move up the ranks of hell, the graver their sin becomes. They drop down to a lower level of hell every time they commit wrongdoing.

Animal experiments have shown that if a mouse receives an electric shock every time it goes to get food, it eventually becomes discouraged, and when the shock reaches a certain level, the mouse gives up trying to get food altogether. It works the same way in hell; the lower the spirits fall, the more they suffer from the weight of their sins. Despite this, some spirits repeat this vicious cycle until they fall into the deepest reaches of hell.

Once they reach the bottom level of hell, they can only find few people. The bottom part of hell seems muddy and thickened with darkness. It's pitch black, so the spirits can't see anything around them. In the end, spirits who continue to commit wrongdoings will be completely secluded in the Hell of Isolation.

9

What Determines Our Destination in the Spirit World?

Gravity Seems to Be at Work in Hell

Hell seems to be under the influence of some form of gravity. The spirits in hell haven't achieved even a basic level of awareness and strongly hold onto worldly values. Most are materialists who believe that this world is everything.

As a basic rule, most people who don't believe in the afterworld and lack faith in God will go to hell. Those who believe in misguided religions or fanatical religious sects will also often find themselves in hell, but the vast majority of those who end up in hell do not believe in the world after death.

Those who do not believe in the other world develop a strong faith in the laws that govern this world. This may be why, when I observe what happens to these people, it seems that gravity operates in hell.

As I've said before, spirits in heaven can fly freely through the sky. Some even have wings to help them fly. In contrast, as far as I can tell, the inhabitants of hell seem incapable of flying. They all walk on the ground.

Spirits in hell can fall down freely; they fall headfirst from cliffs and mountains or nose-dive into holes. But the way they fall is like taking a dive; it's not like flying with complete control. It seems that they can fall down but not fly. So from the way the inhabitants of hell act, they appear to live under the influence of gravity.

Because of this "gravitational force," the deeper they go down in the depths of hell, the darker their surroundings become, and the heavier their bodies feel. This heaviness may be the reason they can't fly.

Having said this, there are evil birds in hell that can fly. We can also find devils that have batwings. Devils that become spiritually powerful can fly, but average spirits in hell can't; they can only walk on the ground, trudge along gravel paths, and climb up hills, sometimes sliding down a slope, just as we do here in the physical world sometimes.

Unlike the spirits in heaven, the inhabitants of hell cannot freely travel through the air, because their level of spiritual awareness is not high enough to understand the laws of the spirit world. So it seems that gravity is at work in hell but not in heaven, where spirits can travel through the sky freely, at will.

☼

Why Does Hell Exist?

From ancient times, people have wondered why hell should exist and why God leaves it untouched. It may be a natural question for people to ask, especially if they are already in hell or near it. But in fact, if we compare the size of the spirit world to a fifty-story building, hell is only the size of the basement. The building may have five basement floors, but there are fifty stories above the ground. This is the basic structure of the spirit world; it predominantly consists of heaven, and hell is only a small part below ground that's only there to keep it in balance.

The fact that the underground part exists shows that there is a passing mark for our spiritual training as children of God and that some people cannot make it. Not everybody can get a perfect score, and not everybody can pass. Those who live in a selfish and egotistical way will face consequences. There is a certain passing mark that's necessary to enter heaven, and those who don't reach it will find themselves in hell.

There is a minimum standard that we, as children of God, need to meet to move up from hell to heaven. There is a certain way of life that we are expected to pursue in this world, and there will always be some who do not clear this minimum requirement. This system lets us polish our souls by learning from one another, although our learning may only be relative. The existence of hell helps us repent and realize where we went wrong.

※

Faith Is a Prerequisite for Entering Heaven

Heaven is made up of worlds on different levels. Just as students are placed in different classes based on the results of their placement tests, spirits in heaven are divided into separate groups and reside on different levels layered on top of one another. In this world, placement tests measure students' academic abilities, but in heaven, it is the level of spirits' faith that determines which level of heaven they should reside in. Spirits in heaven are ranked solely based on their level of faith.

The spirit world consists of different dimensions, from the fourth to the fifth, sixth, and beyond. Each of these dimensions is divided into about three levels, which are further broken down into smaller groups. The spirits in heaven belong to different groups depending on their level of faith.

Hell is essentially a world inhabited by those who do not have religious faith, namely those who hold mistaken beliefs, atheists, and materialists. In addition to those who didn't believe in God, there are hypocrites who acted like they had faith while they were alive, but didn't really believe in their hearts. Those who went to church every Sunday only for the sake of appearances and did not actually believe will also find themselves in hell after they die.

Even temples and churches exist in hell; priests, ministers, and monks who held and taught mistaken beliefs while they were alive engage themselves in religious activities in the shallow parts of hell. In these religious facilities, they give sermons, but there is something wrong with what they are teaching. The hypocrites assemble and listen to these sermons, believing they are leading religious lives, but these people haven't realized the mistakes in their religious beliefs.

The first requirement for entering heaven is faith, which means having a heart that believes in God. We also need to believe that human beings are spiritual existences, that the spirit world is the original world we belong to, and that this physical world is only a temporary abode. Having this basic form of faith is a prerequisite for entering heaven. Once you get there, you will go to a world that corresponds to the level of your faith.

First and foremost, we need to believe. The next step we need to take is to behave in such a way that our deeds, actions, and practices accord with our faith. It's not enough just to believe; our actions need to reflect our faith. As our actions begin to correspond with our faith, we will gradually move up to higher worlds in heaven.

In the Higher Dimensions, Love Becomes a Synonym of Truth

As we go up higher in heaven, we will notice that the spirits we meet have a stronger sense of love and mercy, and we'll find an increasing number of people who selflessly devote themselves to helping others and the world.

In higher dimensions of heaven, the word *love* no longer means love between two people, as in the sense of saying, "I love you" to someone. The word *love* becomes almost a synonym of the word *Truth*. We begin to see that love is Truth and that love is an inevitable rule that we have no choice but to follow once we know the laws of the spirit world governed by God. It is simply impossible to live without following this rule once we understand the laws of the spirit world.

As we move up to the higher worlds of the spirit world, we will see that love and Truth become one and the same. Just as we need to balance ourselves to ride a bicycle, we can't live in a balanced way unless we live by the Truth.

To live according to the Truth is to practice love and mercy.

The inhabitants of hell, on the other hand, think only of themselves. As a matter of fact, those who live solely for their own sakes place themselves at the greatest disadvantage. The suffering and anguish they've caused themselves are preventing them from breaking out of hell.

Those who care only about themselves go to hell, while those who care about others go to heaven. It may seem strange, but it's true: this is the law of action and reaction in the spirit world. Escaping hell is actually very simple; all that the spirits there need to do is to change their mindsets. If only they can change the way they think and their attitudes, they will be able to free themselves from hell.

It is for this reason that at Happy Science, we teach people to practice a love that gives instead of a love that takes, to understand the importance of faith, to treasure others, and to believe in the existence of the spirit world.

Social Status in this World Has Nothing to Do with Our Destination in the Afterworld

There are various ways to measure our status in this world; for instance, social position, income, and academic background. But these worldly factors are irrelevant to whether we go up to heaven or go down to hell, because our destination will be determined based on a completely different set of values.

A typical image of hell that Japanese people had back in the Heian period (794–1192) was that it was a place where demons chased the dead, boiled them in a bubbling cauldron, roasted them over a fire, and ate them. These demons would also shatter people's skulls with clubs.

Today, these demons have been replaced by evil-hearted surgeons, nurses, public prosecutors, judges, and members of the press (although, of course, the majority of people in these professions are good people). In the hospitals of hell, vicious surgeons with mouths torn to their ears kill their "patients" by slicing them up with scalpels, hiding their malevolent grins behind surgical masks.

And the victims go through the endless cycle of being killed and coming back to life.

There are also nurses in hell. Those who worked as nurses but lacked a heart of love when they were alive help the surgeons by kidnapping, incarcerating, and killing their patients. Wicked public prosecutors arrest the dead and find pleasure in tormenting them. Evil police officers also take the place of demons.

A Japanese folktale tells a story about the king of hell, Enma, who is said to be a judge of the afterlife. In fact, judges in the world after death today wear black robes just as they do here. There are judges in heaven as well as in hell—they're people who like sitting in judgment on others.

Judges who hand out wrong judgments that go against their own consciences while they are alive end up in hell. These people stand in judgment over the dead, writing up and reading out death sentences such as "this person is sentenced to be torn limb from limb."

Regardless of our social status or occupation here on Earth, we are divided into two opposite destinations in the afterlife. Doctors exist not only in hell but also in heaven. Surgeons in heaven remove the malignant parts of the spiritual bodies of the souls who have just moved up from hell. They perform operations to remove the part of the astral body that is negatively affected by the person's mental condition.

Nurses in heaven help new arrivals from hell as they undergo rehabilitation. Judges in heaven use the right perspective on life to determine the appropriate destination for each soul. Members of the press who acted on their consciences with an earnest wish to right evil and improve the world write articles for newspapers or broadcast news about events in heaven. There are all types of people that take part in a variety of activities in the spirit world.

We can also find newspaper reporters in hell. These reporters reside in the upper reaches of hell, writing articles for the newspapers published in hell. They write stories about recent arrivals to hell. If they find a newcomer who was a famous figure on Earth, they add a large headline like, "The President of Such-and-Such Company Arrives in Hell Only to Be Knocked Out." They also write follow-up stories to keep readers informed. The headline to a follow-up story may read, "President Impeached and Torn Limb from Limb," "President Burned to Death," or "President Falls to a Lower Level of Hell," depending on what has happened to him.

10

Have a Heart
Fit for an Angel

When we return to the spirit world, we will be judged for all our motives and actions. And we will continue to live in much the same way we do in this world. Those who do not know their inner world will be in big trouble after they die, and that's why I would like these people to open their eyes to the Truths we teach at Happy Science as soon as possible while they are still alive.

This is particularly true of materialists; we need to teach them the Truths and bring about a conversion in their beliefs as quickly as possible. It is very difficult to teach these people the Truths after they've died. Wherever their destination may be in hell, they will most likely stay in one location. Since they have no experience of other places, they don't realize that there are any other worlds besides the one they are in.

We also need to save those who hold mistaken thoughts and beliefs. I earnestly hope that these people can prepare for their entry into heaven while they are still alive. And it is to this end that we need to increase the number of people who have hearts fit for angels.

Further Reading:
J. S. M. Ward's *Gone West: Three Narratives of After-Death Experiences* [London: William Rider & Son, 1918] and G. Cummings's *The Road to Immortality* [London: Psychic Press, 1967] offer views of the spirit world that are similar to the views introduced in this chapter.

CHAPTER TWO

mysteries of the afterlife
Q&A

I

The Difference
between
a Soul and a Spirit

QUESTION

What is the difference between a soul and a spirit?

ANSWER

Souls Continue to Outwardly Express
Their Physical Self-Perception

The terms "soul" and "spirit" both refer to spiritual aspects of ourselves, and in a broad sense, the meaning of the soul is included in the idea of the spirit. But when we speak of a soul, we are more conscious of physical associations with the life the person led on Earth. When a spiritual being appears to us showing many of the individual characteristics it possessed while on Earth, both in appearance and in mentality, you can refer to it as a soul. Put another way, you can think of a spiritual being as someone's soul if it continues to express its individual appearance and personality as it lived on Earth.

Spirits Have Awakened to
Their Spiritual Essence

A spirit, on the other hand, is more spiritually awakened and has surpassed the notion of physical appearance and individuality. Not everyone in the other world undergoes spiritual training in the shape of a human being. The majority of souls in the fourth and fifth dimensions might continue to do so, but those in the sixth dimension and above take on a different appearance.

The sixth dimension is where many souls begin to awaken to their true potential as spirits. They gain a clear understanding that their true essence is not their physiological functions. Much to their astonishment, they discover that their faces, arms, and legs are not really necessary.

In another book, entitled *The Laws of the Sun*, I wrote about this dimension as a world where we are distinguished by the breadth of our knowledge of the Truths, an important measure for setting one soul apart from another. This world contains knowledge about God and the universe God created, and as we learn about these things during our time in the sixth dimension, we begin to intellectually understand that our appearance—as a person with hands, feet, a certain height, and a certain weight—is not truly who we are.

Souls in the Sixth Dimension Train to Overcome Bodily Conceptions

Many people in the sixth dimension can guide your learning and teach you a variety of spiritual practices to help you abandon your physical image. These exercises are sometimes administered by guiding spirits who come to visit from the higher dimensions. They often assemble a group of souls into a gymnasium-like room and ask each soul to come forward and describe what kind of person they were on Earth. After hearing everyone's answers, the guiding spirits ask the group, "Have you read and understood the books and teachings on the possibilities lying within your souls?" To which they all respond, "Yes I have." The guiding spirits reply, "Then we'll try an experiment. You are going to transform yourselves into something other than yourself. Can you give this a try?"

Many souls appear in the other world wearing clothes, but interestingly, they do this so unconsciously that they don't even realize that they're doing it. So this is often where they'll begin their spiritual training. For example, if they happen to have a blue shirt on that day, they'll be asked to turn it into a white shirt. At first, they won't believe that this is possible. But their guiding spirit will reassure them that they can do it and advise them to think very hard about changing their shirt into white. When they do this, they'll see their shirt really turning white. They'll realize to their utter surprise that they have this ability.

In the next step of their exercise, the guiding spirits will tell them, "You are still convinced that you have arms and legs. So now, you'll practice changing your bodily appearance into another image of your choice. Choose anything that comes to mind that you can continuously picture within your mind." When they finish deciding on something, the guiding spirits will remind them of their power to take on that form as long as they earnestly believe that they can. So, if someone were to choose to transfigure into a giant, fifteen-foot-tall sumo wrestler, he would succeed in doing so.

As they do these exercises, souls learn that a higher state of consciousness only becomes possible when they can rid their minds of physical associations with their bodies. When they begin to be able to transform at will, they become capable of living as a spirit.

Spirits Are Shapeless and Intelligent Energy

Tathagatas are spirits who belong to the eighth dimension and embody the spiritual principle "One is many; many are one," and they are able to take on different forms simultaneously. That is to say, one tathagata is capable of showing up as different forms in numerous places to carry out multiple tasks concurrently. This is what we become capable of doing when we attain the consciousness of a tathagata.

One stage prior to this, our soul has to have attained the consciousness of the ability to transfigure ourselves at will, as I described above. We need to have this skill before we can learn to disperse our souls into numerous forms, an ability that represents the true essence of what makes a spirit a spirit. Spirits are originally shapeless and formless; they are purely intelligent energy, and by deepening our knowledge of this truth, we advance toward our spirit form.

Spirits who advance even further from this point will surpass their spirit form and become pure energy. At this stage, a spirit exists not as an entity thought up by any being, but as pure energy that manifests in one form or another to fulfill necessary roles. At times, these manifestations will become completely shapeless; for example, a spirit might manifest as a type of will—perhaps as the light of the will of courage or justice. A spirit could also appear as the power of wisdom. In these cases, they no longer express any semblance of a human being and instead exist only as will. So as our souls continue on the path of spiritual development, we become capable of advancing ever closer toward shapelessness.

It doesn't do justice to tathagatas' true nature to call them spirits. They've attained a much higher state of sublime existence. And each of us human beings was originally created to be such an existence. The reason we undergo constant cycles of rebirth between this world and the other world and aim to advance to higher dimensions is so we can learn just how spiritual our true essence really is.

2

How We Plan for
Our Rebirth

QUESTION

*In one of your spiritual messages, a spirit revealed that
we make our own decisions about our next life on Earth.**
*I would like to know if this is the case with everyone and
whether there is more to how the system of rebirth works.*

---

* This spiritual message was given in 1984 by Murasaki Shikibu, the
well-known Japanese author of the *Tale of Genji*.

ANSWER

Our Rebirth Takes Place
in a Variety of Ways

There is a religion I have heard of that teaches that we all create a life plan before we are born on Earth. Because the followers believe this, they often assume that the bumps they encounter in their lives come from either the flaws in their original life plans or a lack of help from their guardian and guiding spirits.

But in reality, whether someone creates a life plan ahead of time depends a great deal on the advancement of that person's spiritual awareness. Usually, spirits belonging to the higher dimensions lay out their life plans in careful detail, choosing their specific parents, environments, and the professions they'll pursue.

On the other hand, there are people in the fourth dimension who have managed to make it to heaven but still don't realize that they're no longer alive and no longer have physical bodies. Some among them are reborn on Earth without specific parents in mind. When the time arrives for them to be reborn, they enter a kind of sleeping state and are drawn to this physical world by the spiritual vibrations of their parents-to-be. The souls themselves don't know where they're headed.

In comparison, people in the fifth dimension are spiritually aware enough to choose their parents beforehand, and those of the sixth dimension will go further and determine their choice of occupation. In this way, whether you construct a life plan before your incarnation depends on what stage of spiritual awareness you have reached.

A Bureau Helps Coordinate the Rebirths of Modern Souls

Some souls continue to cultivate crops in the spirit world and have long forgotten that the physical world exists. For example, farmers continue to grow tomatoes in their fields and celebrate their harvests. To help these souls continue to gain new soul training in the physical world, officials keep track of souls' reincarnations. When they come across someone who has not been to Earth for a long time, their job is to recommend and make sure that these souls will take on their next life on Earth.

Advanced souls, on the other hand, are already enthusiastic about taking on another rebirth. To apply, a soul sends in an application to the reincarnation bureau, indicating the soul's preferred parents and destination. Bureau officials review all the applications, and the applicants receive counseling on how to improve their life plan so it will help them overcome the tendencies of their mind.

For example, if the official feels that some-one is overreaching herself, he may suggest that she go to her second-choice parents to gain better soul training. It's only natural to want to be born into an ideal environment, but that may not be what's best for our soul training in this world. She may take his advice and modify her life plan.

In this manner, some people look for the best possible soul training for themselves with the aid of an expert and decide which location and parents to go to. So some souls take the ini-tiative to set up their next incarnation, while other souls, like the tomato farmer, need to be instructed to be born again and don't have any specific plan in mind.

In these advanced times, many souls are seeking the chance to experience this world.

There are so many souls that the bureaus are drowning in applications. The ages of hunting and gathering and agrarian life endured for a great deal of human history, but they offered us sparse learning experiences, no matter how often we repeated life on Earth. But now, with the growth of modern conveniences, richer experiences are possible, offering more opportunities for soul training in this world. This is why many souls nowadays want a chance to reincarnate on Earth.

Shinto Souls Go to the Pond of Rebirth

Souls who are acquainted with modern life often use this application method, but those who identify with a time further back in history aren't aware that such a process exists. Some souls who still live the same way they did during the tenth century, for instance, require another way to be persuaded to reincarnate.

For example, Japanese souls from the Shinto group relate better to the idea of the forest of rebirth, sometimes known as the pond of rebirth. This is why Princess Kozakura, who was born in Japan five hundred years ago, mentioned the pond of rebirth in her spiritual message. When Shinto people want to be reborn, they go to the forest of rebirth, where they pray at the local shrine. Then they head to a clearing in the forest, where they find a pond about twenty meters (20 yards) in diameter, located three meters (10 feet) below the edge of a cliff. When they look down into the waters of this pond, they're shown their destination on Earth.

To go forward with this rebirth, they then need to muster the courage to dive into this pond. Some souls become rigid with fear and change their mind. But a guardian or guiding spirit will come to help them reconsider, encourage them to go back to the pond, and help them find the courage to eventually jump. Princess Kozakura has said that the shock they experience when they make this jump erases their memories of past lives.

But there is another reason for this cliff, and that is to test the soul's determination. Being born on Earth always entails the risk of winding up in hell in the afterlife. Life in this world is a journey of harsh soul training. So the cliff has been set there to test the soul's courage to take on this risk.

In this way, different methods of rebirth have been prepared for the souls who were born long ago in history, whereas modern souls are given an application where they can list their first, second, and third preferences. There are a variety of different realms in the other world, and each realm requires a method of rebirth that works well for the souls in that realm. And some souls need others to encourage them to take on another incarnation, while others are already willing to go to their next incarnation.

3

What Our Souls Experience during Organ Donation and Cremation

QUESTION

Do our souls feel pain during organ transplants and cremation?

ANSWER

The Soul Continues to Sense Pain While Connected by the Silver Cord

Attached to each of us behind our head is a spiritual cord called the silver cord that keeps our physical body connected to our soul. As long as our soul and body are linked by this cord, we cannot truly be considered dead, and we have the ability to return to our body during an out-of-body experience during sleep or if we lose consciousness from an injury.

In the medical world, brain death and cardiac arrest are thought to signal death, but true death only occurs when the silver cord detaches from the physical body. This is how real human death occurs from a religious, spiritual perspective.

From the moment you stop breathing, it takes about twenty-four hours, on average, for your silver cord to disconnect from your body. There may be slight individual differences depending on the person, but the usual span of time it takes is about twenty-four hours.

This means that if the deceased are taken to the crematorium too soon after being pronounced dead, their souls will experience such tremendous pain that, in some cases, they may thrash about in agony as their physical bodies are consumed by the flames. For this reason, Japan has a longstanding custom of cremating the deceased one day after the wake. This is a correct custom from a spiritual point of view. We should not send the deceased to the crematorium too soon, to prevent unnecessary anguish from befalling the soul.

In olden times, the custom was not to cremate, but to bury the deceased. This custom arose because, back then, people knew that people's souls could still feel pain for twenty-four hours after death. But the custom of burials was eventually replaced by the practice of cremation to prevent the spread of infectious diseases.

The procedure of organ removal also inflicts anguish upon the soul, at least until the silver cord becomes disconnected. When those who don't believe in spiritual truths or life after death are met with death, they often face terrible confusion when they see their organs being removed. There are actual souls inside hospitals forced to face horrific fear when this happens, because they feel like they're still alive. Because of the terrible fear that they experience, they have difficulty moving on to the afterlife.

I'm sure you can imagine their fear as they are forced to watch their organs taken out of their bodies while they are still connected by their silver cord. It must be a horrific experience to endure. Because they haven't learned about life after death, they are struck by fear, unable to understand what is happening to them or uncertain about how they will live in the afterlife.

In addition to the problems that organ donors experience, our organs themselves, which have consciousnesses of their own, can lead organ recipients' bodies to reject the new organs if these organs' consciousnesses wish to reunite with their original soul. Some organ recipients wind up living short lives in the end for this very reason.

It's Crucial to Know the Spiritual Truth behind Organ Donation

I am not completely against the practice of organ donation and transplantation. This practice can lead to positive outcomes if the organ donors believe in their own spiritual essence, are aware of the pain that the procedure will give them while they are connected by the silver cord, and are still willing to go through with it out of a wish to help others live longer. Even those who know what to expect may experience some pain during the actual procedure, but they can much more easily endure the ordeal. They will also be met with an angel who will come to their aid to offer words of comfort and acknowledgment of this benevolent deed. This angel reassures donors that although they no longer have physical lives and are seeing a lot of damage inflicted on their souls, their souls are still complete and will heal shortly.

At the same time, the patients who receive the organs also need to be grateful for their donors' great sacrifice. Lacking gratitude or mistaking the organ donation for a material exchange could result in complications that could lead to the patient's own death not so far down the road.

In the final analysis, it's risky to carry out organ transplants between people who are completely unaware of the spiritual consequences. Many souls' journeys back to heaven are hampered by this ordeal.

But if the organ donor is aware of the spiritual truth behind an organ removal procedure and the organ recipient and his family are grateful for the donor's sacrifice, it provides a basis of harmony and compassion. This is one way we can help prevent complications, such as transplant rejections, from arising. Having this basis of mutual understanding ensures the success of the transplant. And I believe that surgeons should be able to explain this spiritual truth to their patients and organ donors.

The Soul Has a Multilayered Structure

It may seem like a wonder, but your soul, at first, preserves an exact image of your physical appearance after it leaves your body. So your soul will mirror the loss of your internal organs in the beginning. Initially, your soul retains your body's physical appearance, including your hair, nails, eyes, and even eyelashes, and your soul even has a heart beating in its chest. Even though you no longer require oxygen to live, your lungs' consciousnesses continue to breathe, and the consciousnesses of your other bodily functions also continue to operate as they did when you were alive. But as you develop a deeper understanding of life after death, your soul develops the ability to regenerate and restore your organs' consciousnesses to completeness.

Your soul is made up of many layers, and in a broad sense, it is in the outermost layer of your spiritual body, called the astral body, that your internal organs' consciousnesses are found. This astral body is itself made up of many layers, including the spirit body, which in turn envelops the light-body, a layer filled with even more light than we see in the surrounding layers.

When our souls move on to the worlds beyond the fourth dimension, we eventually cast off and leave behind our bodies' astral layer in the astral realm of the fourth dimension. In the fourth dimension, we often spend about one to three years getting used to the world after death. During this time, our deceased family and friends come to visit and teach us about the afterlife.

After spending some time in the astral realm removing the residue of the physical world, we eventually head back to the realm where we originally belonged, whether it was the fifth dimension, the sixth dimension, or a higher dimension. This is when we cast off our astral bodies, which means that this is also when we leave behind our internal organs' consciousnesses.

You are probably wondering what happens to our astral bodies once we cast them off. There is actually someone in the spirit world who gathers them for other souls to use when they are reborn on Earth.

The ghosts that people often encounter on Earth are souls who were unable to let go of their astral bodies because of an emotional attachment to this physical world. Since these ghosts' astral bodies remain with them, they continue to show signs of bleeding and any injuries they suffered in the physical world. This is why ghosts often appear to have the same physical conditions they were suffering from at the time of their death.

Some of my readers may be considering donating their bodies to scientific research. I think it's fine to do this, but you really must be aware of the truth that we are spiritual beings with souls and spiritual consciousnesses. I can't emphasize enough how much many souls are suffering because of our lack of knowledge of the spiritual truth behind organ donation. When I hear what is happening inside large hospitals through my spiritual eyes and ears, I hear the cries of many terrified spirits. We need to become fully aware of this fact. But as long as we are prepared with the right spiritual knowledge and depth of understanding, we can transform organ donation and transplantation into acts of compassion.

4

How to Recognize
and Deal with a
Negative Spiritual Influence

QUESTION

How can I tell when a pattern of thought is being caused by a negative spiritual influence and when it is coming from a part of my own personality?

ANSWER

The First Step:
Examine Your Visage in a Mirror

A simple way to determine whether you're under a negative spiritual influence is to study your face in a mirror. If you have come under the influence of an evil spirit, you will be able to tell, to an extent, by looking at your face in the mirror. Signs of the quality of our spiritual lives manifest in our countenances very candidly, so if you have been suffering spiritually in your day-to-day life, your face will gradually come to show signs of it. Your visage will begin to resemble beings we often see being pictured with horns, fangs, and tails.

We human beings can have many kinds of negative thoughts, and different kinds of evil spirits correspond to each one. According to the spiritual law that similar vibrations attract one another, evil spirits are drawn to people who express spiritual vibrations like their own but not to people with dissimilar spiritual wavelengths.

For example, people who suffer from aggressive tendencies are prone to attracting spirits with an aggressive quality who live in the Hell of

Strife, but not spirits from the Hell of Lust. It's difficult for a spirit to influence someone with a mismatched spiritual vibration, because it feels uncomfortable being around someone with dissonant vibrations.

It's also true that if you have lived with a negative influence over a long period of time, you may have taken on the evil spirit's tendency of mind as your own. In some cases, people have been living with a negative spiritual influence for ten years or more. These people may find it difficult to tell the difference between their own inner tendency and the spirit's.

When we enter the world after death, we are normally shown our lives played back to us, for example, on a mirror or a screen. This gives us the chance to reflect on the mistakes we've made in our lives and then determine for ourselves which destination in the afterworld we should move on to. However, if your connection with a spiritual influence has grown so close that its tendency has become integrated with you, as though you and the spirit have become one, then you will be sent straight to the world of the spirit's origination, no questions asked.

This usually occurs when we come under the influence of four, five, or more spirits.

If the spiritual disturbance belongs to a devil or demon, you may find yourself, upon your death, immediately wrested away to the world the devil or demon came from. If the evil spirit's influence on you has reached the level of being assimilated with you, you've gone beyond the point where immediate self-examination can help you. Such people have lived lives of inner hell in this world. Hell, in truth, doesn't exist just when we die; it can also exist within our minds while we live through this physical world.

The Second Step:
Gain Knowledge of the Spiritual Truths

If we ever experience a negative spiritual influence, there is a way we can help ourselves realize it's happening, and that's by gaining knowledge of the spiritual Truths. Knowledge of the Truths is the beginning of everything. As we often say, "Knowledge is power," and this pearl of wisdom expresses a genuine truth. By lacking true spiritual knowledge, we allow ourselves to remain powerless.

Knowledge gives us strength; it gives us the power to look before we leap. And if we do end up falling, our knowledge will help us figure out how to heal our wounds. Some people go through life never having realized what is causing their negative tendency, and in the end it doesn't serve them to fault their upbringing, education, or workplace for never having educated them about the spiritual Truths.

So, first and foremost, it is crucial for you to learn the spiritual Truths. This knowledge may open the path to salvation for you. This is why I earnestly talk about the value of spreading and gifting books about the Truths to others. When we make these efforts, we may often encounter opposition. People may tell us to mind our own business, that they found the book offensive, or that they didn't really want to be taken to the local temple. But perhaps those who come to us saying these things are the people who most need to hear the Truths. They may refuse to hear anything about the Truths, but that doesn't change the fact that the Truths are vital to their lives.

We need to begin by learning. Just by reading through this single book, you can make a big difference in your life. It won't take much of your time to finish reading this book. All you need is one day over the weekend to read it from cover to cover. But that one day that you spend reading this book will change your life.

This is why I'm so eager for all of us to devote ourselves to spreading the Truths to more and more people. And for those who have not been introduced to the spiritual Truths before, I would like you to know how vital it is to gain this knowledge while you are still living in this world. Everything in your life will depend on this. Whatever negative spiritual influence you may be experiencing now, your path to recovery can only begin by first learning the Truths. So I hope you'll open your mind to the spiritual Truths that I teach.

The Third Step:
Seek to Acquire the Spiritual Truths

In addition to gaining knowledge of the Truths, we also need to seek to acquire more of the Truths. This desire is referred to in Japanese as *gudoshin*, the "quest for the Truths," or *bodaishin*, an "aspiration for enlightenment." We need to awaken our desire to seek the Truths as our next vital step to overcoming negative spiritual influences.

When you want to introduce people to the Truths, instilling them with a desire to make the Truths a part of their lives is of the utmost importance. But some people who have committed serious misdeeds may need to begin by turning over a new leaf in their attitude. This may require you to stir them into spiritual conversion by speaking words of Truth to them.

If this doesn't turn out successful for these people or for those who just have never encountered the Truths, one or another kind of setback or adversity—such as an illness, injury, a business going under, a divorce, or the death of a loved one—may be lying in wait to help open their eyes to the Truths. Such experiences may be necessary to open the minds of those who refuse to listen to the Truths. All in all, there are two choices: to wait until they are met with adversity or to speak words imbued with the power of the Truths to move them to spiritual conversion.

The premise of my religious organization, Happy Science, is to spread knowledge of the Truths to each person across the globe. This is an aim we cannot shrink away from, no matter what others tell us. We feel that it is our duty and our mission to bring everyone a chance for spiritual awakening.

Those who resist your efforts to introduce them to the Truths and books about the Truths are the ones who truly need them. You could play the role of either the harsh north wind or the gentle rays of sunshine, but whichever approach you choose, persistence will be your key to success.

In the end, missionary work requires this single element: perseverance. It takes time for our progress to appear, but we need to be persistent about continually setting our aims high. This is, indeed, the task that has been set for all believers in Happy Science.

So, in conclusion, my advice to you is to start telling others about the spiritual Truths and then inspire them to seek the Truths for themselves. If you succeed in leading them to the level of knowing and seeking, you will see the rest of the path fall into place smoothly. This is the stage you should reach for in your efforts to lead others to the Truths.

5

The Worlds Where Prominent Poets' Souls Belong

QUESTION

What spiritual level of the other world do poets such as Goethe, Heinrich Heine, and Byron belong to?

ANSWER

Great Poets Have Attained a High Level of Spiritual Awareness

Goethe belongs to the eighth dimension, which is the second-highest level of the human spirit world. In Buddhism, the spirits of this dimension are called tathagatas. Heine and Byron are from the seventh dimension, where the spirits are called bodhisattvas. A well-known Japanese poet, Kenji Miyazawa, is another bodhisattva, and the poets Chuya Nakahara and Michizo Tachihara have not completely achieved this state but are in the close vicinity.*

As you can see, many great poets have attained spiritual eminence in the other world. This is because they possess spiritual minds and have attained a higher level of awareness than spirits who work in other fields, such as the spirits of academic scholars, many of whom reside in the sixth dimension. This is the reason you will find many authors of outstanding poetry coming from the seventh dimension or above.

---

* For more information about the different dimensions of the other world, please refer to the figure on page 31.

Poets are pure of heart, and some have led brief lives in this world, sometimes not even reaching the age of thirty. The hearts of many poets suffer little muddling and are so transparent that this enables the poet to draw inspiration from heaven to compose beautiful works of poetry. In this sense, they have a very spiritual constitution, and this is the reason that so many authors of beautiful poetry have advanced further spiritually than scholars immersed in intellectual study.

When we think of the life that Goethe led, he demonstrated a preeminent gift not only for composing poetry but also in other endeavors, including literature and politics. He was a spirit of vast capacity, the quality that earned him the eminence of a tathagata. Another noteworthy tathagata and poet is Shakespeare, the Bard. Other noteworthy bodhisattvas of the literary world include the great Japanese novelist Soseki Natsume and the master haiku poet Matsuo Basho.

Religious Leaders Guide People with a Heart of Poetry

Because they have progressed so far spiritually, great poets closely resemble religious leaders who possess the power to touch others spiritually through their brevity. In a sense, religious leaders produce the most sublime poetry. We seldom have seen a religious leader who lacked eloquence. Jesus Christ was a true poet, and the same holds true of the Chinese philosopher Chuang-Tzu. The beauty and spiritual resonance of their words have often demonstrated the power to move people's hearts to their depths. In this sense, we can go so far as to say that Jesus Christ was the greatest poet of all time.

Yet another figure who deserves to be considered a superb poet is the Chinese philosopher Confucius. *The Analects*, the Confucian scripture revered by so many, has survived through the ages to this day because of the sublime expressions that resonate through Confucius's words. I think this is why his teachings have been passed down through so many generations up to this very day. I find in the words of *The Analects* the epitome of supreme eloquence.

The value in what's being said is not enough for teachings to survive a span of two thousand years unless the expressions have an eminent quality. True poetry has an element that surpasses time and endures through the ages.

The Japanese Buddhist monk Nichiren is another figure who led many people with a heart of poetry. Others wouldn't have been stirred to take action and follow someone unless the person's words had touched their hearts and moved them in the depths of their soul. This is how poetry has proved to serve a pre-eminent role in the lives of all of us.

6

The Impact of
Scientific Progress on the
Development of Our Souls

QUESTION

I've learned that we can enjoy more freedom when we become souls in the other world. With scientific progress making our lives in this world more convenient and allowing us to live lifestyles similar to those of the other world, how might our soul training in this world change?

ANSWER

Progress in this World
Also Manifests in the Spirit World

There is still quite a gulf between the conditions in which we live in this world and how souls live in the afterworld. But both worlds are undergoing gradual changes that make them more similar—this, at least, is certain to me. Because the two worlds work in close association, when we make our lives in this world more like the lives of those in the spirit world, it can lead the spirit world to progress in tandem. In the same vein, if the progress of this physical world slows down, so will the progress of the spirit world.

In recent times, the spirit world has seen the return of modern souls whose memories of Earth have led the spirit world to modernize. With the newfound freedom these souls gained from their liberation from material fetters, they have recreated in the spirit world much of what they experienced in the physical world.

So, while we often see developments in the spirit world materialize in the physical world, the opposite also holds true: the things we create in this world manifest in the other world. In recent years, an increasing number of souls have reincarnated on Earth, and as a result, the other world is constantly manifesting new developments and bringing modern changes on board. The spirit world is a place that will achieve whatever we modern people can conceive. And whatever we cannot think up, they won't be able to manifest either. This is how these two worlds have been working in association with each other.

Modern Advancements Like Cars and Airplanes Have Also Appeared in the Spirit World

Since the onset of the twentieth century, we have seen numerous people on Earth earning a living in the automobile industry, and souls who want to create automobiles have also appeared in the spirit world. When these souls passed away, they couldn't think of anything to do in the other world but get to work again creating cars. This phenomenon arose from the souls' wishes to continue doing the work they were familiar with.

As many such souls returned and gathered in the afterworld, communities of modern souls who use cars eventually appeared there. There are also former pilots who continue flying airplanes in the spirit world, even though there is no such need in the afterworld. These communities were nonexistent until the nineteenth century arrived.

As you can see, many new lifestyles are being adopted in the afterworld and bringing about cultural changes. Without these changes, modern people in the afterlife would grow bored of the monotony of olden lifestyles. So as more and more modern people arrive in the afterworld, these contemporary souls will build communities that mimic their lifestyles on Earth. This process is what allows the afterworld to continue to change.

The more progress we make in this physical world, the more they'll be inspired in the other world to bring about new advancements like these. So the progress we make in this world will benefit the other world, too.

Repeating Cycles of Rebirth Allows Us to Stay Relevant to Continuously Evolving Times

I have just talked about what happens to contemporary souls in the afterworld, but their presence has brought bewilderment to souls who have lived in the spirit world for hundreds of years since their death. Most people in the after-world lose interest in what's happening in the physical world, except, of course, those who are currently serving as the guardian spirits of people on Earth. So, over the course of hundreds of years, many souls' memories of Earth have faded and have almost completely vanished from their minds. Some may not remember that their country of birth even existed.

When contemporary souls begin forming modernized towns and communities, older souls often think that these newcomers have gone mad and voice their concerns. But modern souls often answer these complaints by saying, "No, we haven't. It's just that you're living in a time so far back in history," leaving little hope for immediate reconciliation. In such cases, contemporary souls may need to recommend that these older souls consider another reincarnation on Earth. In other cases, the older souls themselves may realize how outdated they've become and that they need to gain new experiences through a new incarnation to Earth so they can comprehend the changes going on in their world.

The souls who reside in the upper level of

the World of Light, which is what we call the sixth dimension, are generally aware of the latest developments on Earth, so they don't experience these issues. But those from the middle levels of the World of Light and below are more strongly influenced by and identify with their earthly lives as they lived them, so they aren't aware of how our lives on Earth have changed since then.

So people in the other world need to accelerate their cycles of reincarnation to keep themselves informed about new times. They may find it hard to understand what contemporary souls are doing and talking about and so may be told to be reborn on Earth again. For this reason, many souls have been reincarnating at a faster pace, further accelerating the modernization of the other world.

I am always in contact with various souls of the other world, and those who have just recently returned there are able to understand and explain to me what's going on in the afterworld based on their recent experiences on Earth. Whether they came from Japan or another country, I can talk to these accomplished souls once they return to the spirit world to find out their perspectives on various topics. These conversations allow me to implement their advice into my organization's management.

In conclusion, changes in this world and the other world are closely linked. There is nothing wrong with making progress in this world, and because of our ongoing progress, it's unlikely that our soul training will ever reach full completion. If such a time truly arrives, then it will only be a signal that we should all move on to another planet where new training will await our souls.

7

How Our Souls Evolve through Cycles of Rebirth

QUESTION

How will our souls evolve further as we continue eternal cycles of reincarnation?

Were the ninth-dimensional souls created as highly advanced souls from the beginning, or have they also gone through cycles of rebirth and persevered to reach their current stage of progress?

ANSWER

Ninth-Dimensional Souls Were Created to Be Teachers of Other Souls

To begin with the second part of this question, the spirits of the ninth dimension, numbering ten in all, were mostly created to be teachers of other souls. As I mentioned in another book, called *The Laws of the Sun*, a number of souls have successfully advanced to the eighth dimension, but none have progressed to the ninth dimension.

So what happens to these spirits of the ninth dimension when they continue evolving? When these spirits eventually complete their missions on Earth, they will move on to another planet that suits them to serve as its new leader. This will leave a vacancy on Earth, which will be filled in by an eighth-dimensional spirit.

This is how the process of evolution works in the higher realms of the spirit world. It's like how we, in this world, advance up the corporate ladder. And in the corporate world, when you complete your term, you retire or leave your position. In the same way, when these ninth-dimensional spirits complete their full mission within the training environment of Earth, they often move on to another planet that offers the soul training that they need next. In fact, all ten of Earth's current ninth-dimensional spirits originally came from another planet elsewhere in the universe. After a ninth-dimensional spirit experiences many such transitions from one planet to another, it evolves to the tenth dimension.

Cycles of Rebirth Add Breadth to Our Souls' Experiences

To move on to the first half of this question, which is asking what happens to our souls after numerous cycles of reincarnation, my answer is: it depends on the individual. There's no guarantee of what will happen to any particular individual's soul in the future.

What I can tell you is that when I look at what's happened to various souls so far, I see that there are various degrees of progress. Some have remained at the same level, including those who have gone through many cycles of progress and regress. Others have continued on a down-hill spiral for some time and have stopped only because there is nowhere further down to go.

If we consider Earth's souls from a long-term perspective, however, we see that we've made a lot of progress as a whole. We've spent approximately four hundred million years undergoing soul training on planet Earth, and many teachings have been given to humanity during this time. All those who have learned these teachings and followed them in their lives have gained new wisdom with each rebirth. When we consider these areas of growth alone, there's no doubt that we have all collectively gained something or other from these experiences.

Besides the different degrees of spiritual awareness that different souls have achieved, our souls also vary in their capacities. Even when we fail to progress up the ranks in our spiritual awareness, we can each still broaden the capacity of our soul by enriching ourselves with experiences. By reincarnating on Earth time and time again, we each gather more experiences for our soul. This is another type of soul evolution that we are capable of achieving.

What I have just explained is the process that souls on Earth take to gradually evolve over the course of many cycles of rebirth. And, when, in the middle of this process, a soul sees that it has suddenly progressed, it will move on to another place in the afterworld that better suits it.

Evolved Souls Will Eventually Move On to Other Planets

The population of the physical world has grown to seven billion, and the number of souls in the spirit world has now reached forty-five billion. It's been decided that in about one thousand years, a group of Earth's souls will emigrate to another planet where they can find new opportunities for learning. When this time comes, the souls who have completed most of their soul training on Earth will be departing.

In the same vein, many souls from other planets have immigrated to Earth and are living among us as we speak. They're not just here physically; they've arrived in fleets of souls so they can be born physically as people of our planet. Many of them are experiencing life as a human being on Earth for the very first time.

I won't name any names, but several countries around the world, located both close to and far away from Japan, have experienced rapid population growth, and these countries are hosting many of the souls who are undergoing their first soul training here on our planet. They are now trying to get a sense of what it is like to live on planet Earth.

From a wider perspective, plans for the mass migrations of souls like what I have just described have been set and created to foster the continued spiritual evolution of our souls. What I've described mainly refers to large group migrations of souls, but people's states of mind can vary as individuals, too, based on the efforts each individual has made in his life.

Being Born as an Animal Reawakens Our Appreciation for Being Human

As a basic rule, human souls are born to Earth as humans, but in some exceptional cases, humans are born as animals. There are various types of realms within hell, including the Hell of Animals, also known as the Hell of Beasts, and that's where human souls who've turned into animals are.

In a novel by the author Ryunosuke Akutagawa called *Toshishun*, there are people who've fallen to this realm of Hell, including the parents of the main character, Toshishun, and some of them are described as having the bodies of horses.

In reality, many souls there have fully taken on the appearance of animals, including even their faces. After having spent hundreds of years there, they have gradually forgotten that they were human beings to begin with and now believe in their hearts that how they appear is who they really are. To find relief from their suffering, they come to shrines and temples on Earth seeking people's prayers to soothe them.

Other people in this realm, who have spent many years purifying their minds of resentment and chagrin, have mostly made up for their misdeeds, but some among these still remain forgetful of their sense of worth as human beings. Some of them will eventually be born on Earth to spend one to two years gaining soul training as animals living alongside people, for example as farm animals.

Deep in their hearts, they hold faint remembrances of originally being human, so going through life on Earth in an animal's body can give them a very different experience. If you've ever seen a dog or cat that seems to understand what you think or behaves in especially human ways, it may have originally been a human soul.

What this experience gives the soul is the realization of the value of being born as a human being. After spending time as an animal, the soul will be reborn as a human, but this physical experience as an animal beforehand helps the soul regain an appreciation of life as a human being. Over the course of many incarnations as human beings, some people forget to appreciate the value of being human. But by experiencing life as animals, they rediscover the joys of human life, such as the ability to speak, write, and move around freely. But I should mention that those who have reached this point in the first place have regressed very considerably in their soul training.

Spiritually Advanced Animal Souls Can Evolve into Human Souls

The reverse case, in which animals' souls evolve into human souls, is also possible. This is a natural part of the course of spiritual evolution, which is one of the guiding principles of the universe.

The souls of animals can progress to various levels. As you may have guessed, mammals can be said to have advanced further in their soul training than amphibians and reptiles. And if we look further into the class of mammals, we may find that groups of them that have experienced domestication or have lived by peoples' sides often show human-like emotions, which is a sign of a higher level of spirituality.

For example, tigers and lions, which belong to the cat family, live in the wilderness, but they will be reborn as cats when their souls have progressed far enough. In the same way, wolves will be reborn as dogs. To these souls, reaching the stage of a cat or dog is a tremendous spiritual milestone. To advance further and become human souls, however, they need many more years of repeated cycles of rebirth to deepen their understanding of how humans live and feel emotions. Dogs like Lassie and Hachi, who have evolved so far that they have become heroes in the world of animals, will eventually earn the chance to evolve into human souls.

There is a god in the sixth dimension who is responsible for overseeing animals' cycles of rebirth. This is the god who decides when an animal's soul has advanced far enough to be worthy of living as a human soul. This transformation from an animal soul to a human soul confers a change in the basic nature of the soul.

Opportunities for
Spiritual Growth Know No End

If we humans were to live in another plan-etary being's physical body, we would no doubt gain new experiences for our soul. Some beings from outer space have six arms or are only one meter (3 feet) tall or are giants. Living in such a different physical body naturally leads to a different kind of soul training. It's difficult to say how much soul evolution these experiences could lead us to, but it's at least certain that we'd be able to add breadth to the experiences of our souls. For if we continue the cycle of rebirth eternally, we'll be given eternal opportunities for soul training. This is the secret behind the lives of the soul.

CHAPTER THREE

modern developments
in the spirit world

My Discussion with My Late Father about the Construction of Happy Science Temples in Heaven

My Father's Spiritual Communications with Me After His Death

In this chapter, I would like to share some personal anecdotes about my recent experiences with the spirit world. I have been told, several times, that readers gain a better grasp of my talks when I tell stories about what I have seen and gone through in the other world. Although these are normal occurrences for me, they may not be for my readers. So its difficult to know what will draw peoples interest.

Let me start by talking about my experience when my father, Saburo Yoshikawa, who had been an honorary advisor of Happy Science, passed away on August 12, 2003. It was then that my contact with the spirit world grew more frequent, and I had various kinds of spiritual experiences. From the very beginning of his life in the other world, he had shown an eager interest in giving me spiritual messages from heaven. But I asked him to give himself an opportunity to gather experiences in the afterlife first. Only about three to four months later, however, he came back to see me again, clearly unable to wait much longer to deliver his messages.*

My Father Appeared in One of My Mother's Dreams

During those several months, while my father was undergoing training in the spirit world, my mother was anguishing over my father's absence from her dreams in this world. She couldn't help but worry about him and wonder, "Why hasn't my husband appeared in my dreams at all? It's common for a loved one's spirit to come back to talk to you when they pass away, but not once have I seen or heard from him since the

---

* Later, these spiritual messages were published in Japan in four separate volumes. Ryuho Okawa, *Yoshikawa Saburo no Reigen: Kiten Seppo Vol. 1 to 4*, [Spiritual Messages from Saburo Yoshikawa: Memorial Lectures, Vol. 1 to 4] (Tokyo: IRH Press 2004 - 2006).

day of his death. I wonder what is keeping him. Where could he have gone off to?" But as I said earlier, he was very preoccupied by his spiritual training somewhere in a high place in heaven.

In early December, several months after his death, my father finally received permission to give his spiritual messages and came to see me again. So we proceeded with tape-recording them. I made copies of the tapes and mailed them to my mother in my hometown in Shikoku so she could hear them too. As it turns out, my father finally appeared in one of my mother's dreams around the same time that I'd been recording these spiritual messages.

Her dream had felt very real to her, she told me. During her dream, she saw a high-end black sedan pull up in front of their house. When the door swung open, she saw my father step out of the vehicle dressed in the full style of traditional Japanese attire. She had never seen him dressed so well in this style before, because he never used to wear a customary gentleman's kimono such as this one.

With an air of self-confidence and a bold stride, he came into the house to talk to my mother. He said to her, "If you will take a good look at me right now, you can clearly see that I am as fit as a fiddle. Everyone seems to talk of me as if I don't exist anymore. But I won't let them believe that for much longer. As you can tell, I am perfectly full of vitality." This was the message that my father gave my mother in her dream.

A day or two later, the spiritual message arrived in the mail, and she realized that the spiritual message and her dream had coincided perfectly. This kind of phenomenon, when different people unknowingly experience similar events at the same time, is well-known in psychology and is referred to as synchronicity.

My mother's dream was probably a sign from my father assuring her of his imminent return to work. These were the spiritual events that my mother and I experienced back in December 2003.

☼

My Father and I Discussed Our Temple's Progress in Heaven

In another episode related to this one, in the middle of the night in January 2004, at around two o'clock, I traveled out of my physical body to visit the spirit world. My father met me there and showed me the progress he had made so far. He took me to the Happy Science temples that have been under construction in the fifth dimension, which are most likely intended for the believers of our faith.

There, among the gently rolling hills and fields of green spreading out before me, stood two large buildings. One was on slightly higher ground than the other, and a corridor had been built to connect the two buildings. The exterior of this corridor looked to be constructed of a chalky, cement-like material, and the walls from the waist level and above were made of patterned glass. The corridor looked almost complete, but the rest of the buildings were unfinished. I noticed that these temples resembled our temples in this physical world but we don't have one exactly like it.

My father and I spoke in the corridor, where he pointed out to me several issues with the temples: "The construction of the buildings has progressed, and we are supposed to hold seminars there in the future, but you have been too busy with your work in the physical world to plan these seminars." I had to admit that this was true; I hadn't yet given much thought to these seminars and programs.

Clearly consternated by the lack of directions and outlines for future seminars, he continued: "Since the buildings are still being constructed, no one has come for any seminars yet, but I am wondering what to do when the buildings are finished and ready to open. We are offering many seminars to the people on Earth, but I wonder if there are ones that we can use here. Since no one lives in a physical body anymore, I feel that this matter needs your direct attention."

I realized that he was making a very valid point. It was true that I hadn't considered what kinds of seminars we should offer in the after-life, and it's also true that there will be increasing demand for these seminars in the near future.

※

My Father Was Concerned about Not Being Able to Make Seminars Available

My father raised a second issue about our temples in the spirit world. He wanted to know if there was anyone who was capable of managing the temple's operations and running the seminars. He explained to me, "Apart from me and two other men who have served as senior lecturers* of Happy Science,† there is no one else to administer the seminars. But even they are still undergoing additional training in the spirit world, and while they are on the path to angel-hood, they still have some ways to go to complete their training. I feel uncertain about whether we'll be able to manage everything as we are now. So not only do I see challenges with the temples' administrative needs; the lecturers might also need more time to develop their abilities, and on top of that, the seminar materials haven't been prepared."

In response to his concerns, I told him, "We will just need to wait a little longer until more lecturers come of age and return to the other world, which may take another twenty years. In the meantime, can you welcome the believers who arrive with some friendly conversation over tea or coffee?" It was clear in my mind that we would have difficulty providing them with any seminars until a later time.

When I said this to my father, he was visibly disgruntled. He's rather a perfectionist, so he

---

* I talk about them in more detail in chapter four.

† Here, he is referring to Tamio Kageyama, a well-known Japanese author, and Koji Nanbara, a well-known Japanese actor, both of whom have been deceased.

must not have liked the idea of opening a temple when the temple can't yet offer the believers anything to do. Perhaps the only thing we can have them do is walk through the mountains, while offering the temples as a place to rest. But even then, while much of the exteriors looked finished, construction of the prayer halls hadn't even begun yet. The corridor and the accommodations were the only parts of the temples that had been completed.

Perhaps the only other alternative is to invite someone from the higher realms to serve as a guest lecturer. But, since Happy Science is a new religion, we want to avoid bringing in people from bygone eras so we don't wind up creating old-fashioned cultures and methods.

As you can tell, even in the other world, people often run into issues figuring out how to operate and prepare temples when they are trying to create something completely new. It is also difficult for someone of this world to make decisions about what we want to offer in the other world. So, while we endure the shortage of lecturers, I would like to ask those returning to the afterlife to enjoy taking in the scenery and keep yourselves informed about new developments on Earth. I think that if you give us two to three decades, we will be able to offer seminars at various temples in the other world.

2

The Goddesses of Beauty Set Today's Leading Fashion Trends

The Goddesses Showed Me a New Vision of Beauty

The third spiritual experience that I would like to share occurred on another January day. In this experience, I was taken to a mountainous region of the spirit world, where I was accompanied by an elderly guide. He looked to me to be someone of German descent and had balding silver hair and a silver beard and held a walking stick.

After climbing up a mountainous trail for a while, the scenery began to change, revealing terrains made of crystal. I saw that along both sides of our trail, there were tall, pointy, hexagonal crystals emerging out of the ground where you would normally find trees. Eventually we reached a resting area, and when my guide suggested that we take a break for something to eat, I agreed. I saw that we were probably still near the German spirit world, because the people who came out to serve us were charming, gnome-like people who served us stew and various other dishes.

When we finished our break, we set out on our journey again. And gradually, I saw that the scenery around us was changing further, revealing entire mountains made of pure crystal that kept changing colors into different gradations of the rainbow. When we eventually arrived at a basin, I began to wonder what kind of world this was. I had never been to a place like this before.

Just as I had this thought, there emerged before us four very beautiful women who began to dance. In the olden days, I would have told you that this was the dance of the ancient goddesses, but these women were not dressed in a traditional style. Instead they wore modern-style dresses like you would see in the latest Paris collections today. They introduced themselves to me as the goddesses of beauty, and I recognized one of them as the goddess Aphrodite, but who the other three goddesses were remains a mystery to me.

Each of their dresses was of a different color that gradated in sync with each twirl and spin. If one of their dresses was originally yellow, it would gradate into blends of aqua, pink, and purple as the goddess spun around, and these shifting colors reflected off the transparent crystals that stood tall around them like pillars. What I saw was a whole scenery of constantly shifting colors that blended into one another and changed as the goddesses danced.

It was an incredibly beautiful sight revealing a marvelous sense of color that I had not known to exist anywhere before. As the colors of the goddesses' dresses reflected off of one another and onto the crystal forests, it was as though I was watching the light of a prism emanating a mystical array of tones, many of which were impossible to describe in words known to this world.

※

The Goddesses Inspire
this World through Designers Shops

For a while, I simply stood there in the wonderment of their dance. Eventually, I asked them a question: "Can you tell me what kind of world this is?" "This is the world of the goddesses of beauty," they said. Since I had already guessed as much and wished to know more, I insisted that they tell me more about their roles. In response to my curiosity, one of them stepped forward and offered to show me around their world.

She explained to me that the crystal basin where they had been dancing led to numerous places on Earth. As I followed her, I saw many gates leading from the goddesses' world to various places in the physical world. The gate that we chose to take led us to the luxury boutiques of a large hotel, the kind with exquisite jewelry, scarves, accessories, fashions, and fragrances by designer brands such as Chanel and Hermes. I recognized spiritual routes like this in several hotels, including one that was very familiar to me. I was surprised to learn that the designer brands in pursuit of supreme beauty in fine hotels around the world are connected with the goddesses of beauty through spiritual pathways.

I once wrote, in a series of books titled *Love Blows Like the Wind*,* about the spiritual world of the mermaids who live in a lake that leads to all the seas of the physical world. I learned that the realm of the goddesses of beauty works in much

---

* This series of books was published by IRH Press in Japan. Ryuho Okawa, *Ai wa Kaze no Gotoku*, Vol. 1 to 4 (Tokyo: IRH Press, 1994).

the same way. They have gates that lead to the designer shops that represent beauty in our physical world, and there they inspire people with their visions of beauty.

Most of the stores the goddess took me to did not belong to Japanese designers, but perhaps I would have found some if I had looked more closely.

In this way, the goddesses are able to come and go as they wish to inspire those in this world with beauty. This was the first time I had ever seen their world, so this was also a new discovery for me. We didn't explore any other places, but I'm sure there must also be passageways to the leading designers and fashion models of our time.

It was interesting to learn that there are spirits in the other world who work this way. When I saw that the goddesses wore modern dresses rather than the dresses of ancient times, I understood that they have been the sources of inspiration for those who create beautiful products on Earth. Each season's leading styles and fashion trends are based on concepts these goddesses come up with and send out as spiritual inspirations.

I think it's rare to receive an invitation from the goddesses of beauty, even for me, and to witness the rare beauty of all those gradating and reflecting colors. I was amazed to discover that such a world of beauty exists. And while I didn't think of it at the time, a similar world of fragrances might also exist someplace in the spirit world where spirits devote themselves to producing exquisite blends of perfumes.

3

My Experience of Being Honored as the Sun God

My Visit to the Indian Gods in Mount Meru

In another experience in the month of January, I was taken to yet another part of the spirit world. What was different this time was the very fast speed at which my out-of-body experience occurred. I was flying at such a fast pace that I could hear the roar of the wind in my ears as I traveled higher and higher. And eventually, while I was thinking about how quickly I was traveling and wondering where I was being taken, a large mountain came into sight.

It resembled the Himalayas, which stand tall and are also wide at the foot, but this mountain I saw in the spirit world was slightly taller and narrower. It towered so high, in fact, that I couldn't guess its true height. But because its base was relatively narrow, I could see that it was definitely tall and slender.

Then, before I knew it, I was flying vertically up the side of the mountain at a very fast speed, and I couldn't help but wonder how high I would go and what the name of this mountain was. It was then that I heard the voice of a spirit tell me, "This is the legendary mountain Mount Meru."

According to legend, Mount Meru is a mountain in India, but it doesn't exist in this world. People have suggested that Mount Meru may be one of the peaks in the Himalayan or Kunlun mountain ranges, since both are near India, but the truth is that Mount Meru exists only in the spirit world.

Judging from my own observations, Mount Meru is an extremely tall, pointy mountain— I'd guess that it's well over ten thousand meters high, although it wasn't snowcapped. On my way to the top, I flew past many rings of clouds representing the different realms where the gods live. This was where the Indian spirit world could be found, and I met many famous Indian gods during this journey. Living here and there were many that I recognized and recalled learning about, so I went to pay my respects and speak with each of them. After meeting with each god or goddess, I moved up to an additional level above him or her. I made my journey upwards in this fashion, flying higher and higher.

The Indian Gods Bestowed
Their Highest Honor on Me

I eventually reached the summit of the mountain, where I could find nowhere farther up to go. As I stood there, I wondered to myself, "Could this be the end of my journey, or could there actually be more?" Then, to my surprise, I found myself in the middle of a ceremony being held in my honor.

First, they gave me Indian clothing with a red and yellow design against an olive green background. When they finished dressing me in this outfit and draped the mantle over my shoulders, the coronation ceremony began. They placed a crown on my head that I wasn't able to see for myself, and they handed me a jeweled staff.

When I asked them what this ceremony was for, they told me, "The Indian spirit world has officially recognized you as the most venerated of all Indian gods." This experience reminded me that I had not thought about India's pantheon of gods for some time, but they seemed to have acknowledged and celebrated me as the greatest among them regardless.

In the Hindu religion, the Buddha* is treated as only one of many gods. The Buddha is known simply as one of the ten avatars of Vishnu, a principal Hindu god. Put another way, Hindu theology accorded the Buddha the same level of importance as many other gods. But this is no longer the case, because the deities have celebrated me as the most superior god of all.

They called me by a name I can no longer recall, and though it was not the name "El Cantare," I remember that it meant "God of the Sun," so the name was most likely "Surya." This name probably refers to the sun that can be seen over the summit of Mount Meru. They must have thought that this was a befitting title to grant someone who has reached the highest point in the Indian spirit world.

I felt that this was a rare experience representing a good omen—a sign that the Indian gods are watching and supporting me. The Indian gods very rarely appear among the guiding spirits of Happy Science, but I believe that they accepted me into their spirit world because of my connection with India in a previous life.

---

* Shakyamuni Buddha is a past incarnation of Ryuho Okawa.

4

Our Work Has an Impact on the Spirit World

A Happy Science Spirit World Is Emerging

As you can tell, the spirit world is a mystical world of countless deities who are known by their people as gods, buddhas, or angels, according to their faith or culture. Over the course of thousands or even tens of thousands of years, these gods have gone to many parts of the physical world to found religious faiths and cultures. These faiths then began to emerge in the other world, where the deities have continued to guide believers who return there for their afterlives and gather together in towns and villages. At the moment, Happy Science is a newly formed religion with very few believers in the other world, but we are also sure to see a Happy Science spirit world emerging there in the course of time.

Having a faith is, in truth, a contract. So by believing in a religion during your life in this world, you are ensuring your return to the spirit world that belongs to your choice of faith. When you arrive in the other world, the gods, buddhas, or angels of your faith will come to give you support. They will look after you and offer you guidance on your life plan for your next incarnation on Earth.

In this way, the other world is composed of various spiritual realms, and many souls continue to reincarnate within the spiritual community they've belonged to in the past. But in recent times, we've seen a strong trend toward crossing boundaries internationally. Happy Science in particular has been a force for creating connections across borders, and these international connections have led to a wider recognition of our religion throughout the spirit world.

As I mentioned earlier, the Indian spirit world has given us its stamp of approval. But in the near future, we will also need to win the recognition of the Middle Eastern and African spirit worlds. So we need to develop ways to guide them based on the Truths. And while the Asian spirit worlds will probably accept us rather quickly, historical barriers between the East and West have accumulated over many years and may mean that we'll need additional time to spread into the Western areas of the afterworld. This work arises from our wish to fulfill Happy Science's ideal and true mission: to bring happiness to all.

☼

Change Manifests Mutually in this World and the Spirit World

Just as we at Happy Science continue to build temples, gain new believers, and spread our faith throughout this world, we are also striving to accomplish these things in the spirit world. In the spirit world, people who lived hundreds or thousands of years ago on Earth lived under different cultures and lifestyles from the ones we're familiar with. So it may prove difficult to instill change among these spirits and lead them to accept new ideas.

But this world and the other world are closely linked and constantly influence each other, bringing concurrent changes to bear fruit in both worlds. For example, the descriptions of hell and the other world that the Buddhist monk Genshin (942–1017) depicted during the Heian period of Japan in his treatise, *Ojo Yoshu* ("*The Essentials of Salvation*"), no longer give us an exact portrayal of the other world. Since his time, many people who experienced modern times on Earth have returned to the afterlife and created new spirit worlds, leading to many changes there. These new spirit worlds have influenced neighboring spirit worlds and have spread change more widely throughout the afterworld.

At present, the Happy Science spirit world is predominantly based in the Japanese spirit world, but this is essentially because our activities have been most vigorous in Japan. In actuality, Happy Science's awareness extends farther, on a worldwide scale. Many parts of the spirit world have been limited to their own country or ethnic group, but our activities have been aimed at influencing even these communities and are on the brink of shaking up their commonly accepted notions and beliefs.

Happy Science has continued to expand glob- ally and spread the Truths internationally by conducting missionary work, opening temples worldwide, and publishing books of Truths in multiple languages. When these efforts succeed in extending our reach to a certain degree, a Happy Science spirit world will emerge in the corresponding parts of the other world. It is difficult to say exactly how much the Truths will need to spread for this to happen. But wherever

Happy Science has many believers, a Happy Science spirit world is certain to actualize.

For example, if we succeed in attracting a large group of believers to our faith in a Christian country, a spirit world will appear there that accords with our success. This will invite those of the Christian spirit world who sympathize with our teachings to come to our aid. Then, as our believers on Earth eventually pass on to the afterlife, our faith will spread even further. The same holds true with our activities in the Islamic worlds of the afterlife and in many other parts of the other world.

Earlier, I talked about the spiritual connection that links the goddesses of beauty with the designer stores of fine hotels. The same principle can hold true for the Happy Science spirit world. We can create a grand spiritual network and further succeed in growing our faith by creating a huge Happy Science spirit world in the place that corresponds to the main base of faith in this physical world and by expanding our branches and temples worldwide and thus also developing Happy Science spirit worlds that correspond to those parts of the physical world. This is the vision that we eagerly look forward to fulfilling.

☀

My Aim Is to
Bring Religious
Innovation to Both Worlds

One of my missions in life is to modernize the religions of this world. I also hold a corresponding mission: to modernize the spirit world. Many people have ideas about the spirit world that are two to three thousand years old or even older and support cultures and lifestyles that were established by religions back then. I feel that my purpose in life includes the important work of bringing change to these dated beliefs, reforming the spirit world, and bringing innovation to the religious cultures of this world to better suit the lives of modern people.

In these modern times, we have seen people withdraw from churches and find escape in the pragmatic beliefs of science, hoping they won't have to live in a world where everything is determined solely by the church. The trend has been to think that the further removed you are from religion, the more advanced and modern you'll be. It's now a commonly accepted notion that religion was for people of the ancient world and science is the true answer for our modern world.

But that's not what religion truly is. The true purpose of religion is not to foster a revival of ancient ways. Happy Science is a new religion that is creating a modern religious culture that supports the new lifestyles of people in this age. Happy Science aims to bring religion and science together. Our goal, therefore, is to lead both this world and the next world toward innovative change wherever change is needed, and this is the purpose and basis of our activities.

One of the aims I have talked about repeatedly is to shift the Islamic world in a more modern direction, and the same holds true for India. The ancient Indian religions continue to influence their country to such a strong degree that they have posed a barrier to modernization.

For example, the people of India today continue to worship Ganesha, a god with a human body and an elephant's head, and still also practice *linga* worship, a form of phallus worship, in the same way that some people in Japan used to worship the snake god or forked trees. There is much more to religious faith than these forms of worship. People in India will benefit from knowing that there is a new form of religious belief.

Ultimately, the work we do to spread our faith and expand our horizons will affect the world on more levels than we can fathom right now. What we at Happy Science accomplish in this world will also create change in the spirit world. This power of mutual influence is a spiritual truth that everyone in this world will benefit from knowing. In the end, what we accomplish and create in this world will sync with and manifest in the world of the afterlife. I hope that many people will take to heart the spiritual truths I have talked about in this chapter.

a departure for the afterworld

I

We Will All Face the World after Death

The Questions of Birth, Aging, Illness, and Death Led the Buddha to Seek Enlightenment

In 2004, I published a book called *The World of Eternal Life*,* which focuses on essential issues relating to the transition from this world to the world after death. *The World of Eternal Life* answers the question that drove Gautama Siddhartha (Shakyamuni Buddha) to leave his home, renounce worldly life, and embark on the quest for enlightenment: why do human beings suffer the four pains of birth, aging, illness, and death? Here, let me briefly mention where he was born and preached his teachings.

Shakyamuni was born in the garden of Lumbini near Kapilavastu, in the center of the

---

* This is an English translation of the original Japanese title, *Eien no Seimei no Sekai*, [Tokyo: IRH Press, 2004]. This book is not currently available in English.

Indian Subcontinent, while his mother was traveling back to her parents' home for his birth. Lumbini is now part of Nepal, near the border with India, and the ruins of Kapilavastu are in both Nepal and India. So these two countries have been arguing over which country hosts Buddha's birthplace.

Based on modern geography, his birthplace seems to be situated in the area on the northern edge of India, but because in those days India covered a greater area than it does now, people at that time seemed to consider the area as part of central India. After Shakyamuni renounced worldly life and became a religious teacher, he actively preached his teachings in Magadha, Kosala, and other regions along the Ganges River, which were typically recognized as central India.

According to tradition, what led Shakyamuni to set out in search of religious enlightenment was this question about the meaning of the four pains—birth, aging, illness, and death. He wanted to know why people are born, grow old, get sick, and die. In other words, he questioned the very essence of human life. Shakyamuni left everything he knew in search of the answer to this question. In *The World of Eternal Life*, I use a variety of different approaches to offer answers to this question.

※

The Transition to the World after Death Can Be a Source of Happiness

In the first chapter of *The World of Eternal Life*, I talk about the mysteries of life and equality under death. It is 100 percent true that all of us will eventually die. No one can escape death. To put it another way, we should build our outlook on life with a conscious awareness of our mortality. We should decide how we are going to live our lives based on the premise that death is inevitable.

As I have repeatedly said, the world after death does exist, without a doubt. I can say this with certainty, because I myself have experienced the reality of the world after death on numerous occasions. Stories about the world after death only have the ring of truth when they come from someone who has actually experienced it first-hand. So I hope to use every available opportunity to tell others this truth.

When we humans come into this world, we often develop a strong attachment to our physical life and a desire to live up to two or even three hundred years, if possible. But if we did live that long, we would most definitely find our life very difficult. We would be left with a painful feeling of grief and sorrow as we experienced the deaths of all our friends and loved ones.

Our lives in this world, our human experiences, are ultimately memories of our lifetimes. If our minds remain filled with old memories, we will find it increasingly difficult to adapt and respond to the demands of modern life.

As we get older, we start to forget recent events while retaining clear memories of things that happened decades ago. For example, we can remember things that happened when we were young or tell stories about our children when they were little. Although we can recall events that happened thirty, forty, or even fifty years ago as if they were yesterday and talk about them over and over again, when it comes to things that happened during the last ten years, our memories become rather hazy. This is a common phenomenon among the elderly.

Death feels tragic, but from a higher perspective, we can see that physical death allows us to move on to the next world. So in this context, death can be a source of happiness.

☼

Abortion Causes Confusion in the Lives of Many People

Human beings are born crying and die crying. Even the people who see them off cry. But often they cry because they misunderstand the truth about birth and death. If you think about it, doesn't it seem strange that babies are born crying? It would make just as much sense for them to be born delighted and smiling, but for some reason, babies cry when they are born.

Let me tell you why. Before being born into this world, babies have to endure nine months of darkness and loneliness inside the mother's womb. So babies cry out of relief and joy at being released from their fear, anxiety, and uncertainty about whether they will be safely born into this world.

In fact, they have been feeling insecure since before they entered the mother's womb. From the moment they began preparing in heaven to be born to their promised future parents, they have been worried about whether they will be able to come out into this world without any mishap.

Today, an increasing number of abortions have become a big concern for souls that are planning to be born. Even if their prospective parents make a promise, they may decide to abort the child when it enters the womb. So these souls can't be sure whether they will really be able to come out into this world.

The mother may decide to terminate her pregnancy because she wants to focus on her career or because the father says that he doesn't want any children. The child's soul may call out to them, begging them to reconsider, but its voice cannot be heard.

Abortion is one of the main factors contributing to the current low birth rate and population decline in Japan. So if we can reduce the number of abortions, we can probably solve this social problem. Japan has had a long tradition of infanticide as a result of extreme poverty and an inability to provide for children. Because of this tradition, Japanese women may regard a fetus as just another bodily organ that they can remove if necessary. This may be why some mothers do not think that abortion can have grave consequences and so do not suffer much guilt for having abortions.

But in fact, abortion has become a serious problem that has brought confusion to the lives of many souls. Of course, there are cases when the parents have no choice but to have an abortion. In the case of a loving couple, however, it's best if they can give birth and raise their children if possible.

Nowadays, raising a child is estimated to cost at least one to two hundred thousand dollars, but this is not a prohibitive figure. I hope that, if the parents love each other, they will choose to give birth to their children. I am sure those who are waiting to be born feel the same way.

☀

Departing from this World is Like Entering a New School

As I have said, we cry when we are born into this world, and when we die, everyone around us will cry, too. Not only humans, but also animals seem to mourn death. Why do we feel sad when we face death?

During the several decades that we live in this world, we often find our lives here unexpectedly comfortable and become attached to them.

When the time comes for us to leave this world, we feel sad because we miss the houses we lived in, our families and friends, and various other things that we have developed a liking for.

Transitioning to the afterworld is like entering a new school. It's a process similar to the one we go through when we move up from kindergarten to primary school, although there is a little more disconnection between the two.

You may have heard stories about what happens after death, but you won't be able to completely believe them until you experience it yourself. Listening to stories about life after death is like hearing about the primary school you will be attending. You won't really know what it is like to attend primary school until you put on your new uniform, put your backpack on your shoulders, go through the school gate, and sit in your classroom surrounded by other students.

In much the same way, even if you've heard or read about the world after death, it may not seem real to you. You probably feel like a child who has been told that he is registered to begin school next month but doesn't know exactly what to expect. It's only natural to feel this way. Having lived in this world for several decades, you have simply forgotten the values of the afterworld, the world you originally came from. Although this is inevitable, it is essential that we always keep in mind the Buddhist perspective: the afterworld is the real world where we originally lived, and this world is simply a temporary abode where we stay for several decades.

☼

Be Prepared to Face Death at Anytime

From the Buddhist perspective on enlightenment, the ideal state of mind is to live your life always prepared to die at any moment. Shakyamuni Buddha repeatedly taught that this world is a transient place and that we never know when we may have to leave and return to the world we originally belong to. So he taught again and again that we should cast aside our attachments to this world and live our lives in a way that will leave us with no regrets.

When we face the spiritual reality of life and death, we keenly feel how true his teachings are. I don't think there is any religion other than Buddhism that explains so clearly how attachment to our worldly lives impedes our passage to the afterworld. There are countless religions that teach faith, but only Buddhism has taught the spiritual truth of life and death so explicitly.

Nearly 2,500 years have passed since the time of Shakyamuni Buddha. But when we look at the lives and deaths of a variety of people, we can see that this teaching—that our attachments impede our transition to the other world—is still true today.

By training our minds to cast aside all attachments to this world and achieve inner peace, we can enter the world of nirvana. Those who do not go through this spiritual training will find it difficult to let go of their attachments to this world and will be unable to move on to the next world smoothly.

One question you can ask to see whether someone is likely to end up in hell is "Do you find it impossible to believe in the existence of the world after death?" Put another way, would you be in trouble if the other world existed? If you have no problem with the existence of the other world, you have probably been living right. But if, when you look within and reflect on yourself in conscience, you feel troubled and distressed at the possibility of the existence of the afterworld, then you may find yourself in deep trouble after death. I highly recommend that you start practicing intense and strict self-reflection, because otherwise you may face a very tough time when you begin to repent your actions once you reach the world after death.

Awakening to the truth about the spiritual world in this three-dimensional material world is far more valuable for the soul than engaging in spiritual discipline after you have died and entered the spiritual world. Believing in something that you cannot see with your eyes and grasping the truth while you are still living in this world is a precious lesson that you can learn through your spiritual training in this lifetime. So it's best if you can absorb this invaluable lesson while you are still living in this world.

This simple message is what Buddhism teaches through its numerous sutras. Unfortunately, many Buddhist scholars and monks do not understand this basic and simple truth, because they are unable to change their fixed perceptions. If they would like to grasp this truth, they will need to completely shift their secular view of the world.

☼

Your Life in this World
Will Be Assessed After Death

Buddhism has repeatedly taught that all worldly things are transitory and that this world is only a temporary abode. This means that the other world is the world we originally came from and this world is a place we are merely visiting for a temporary stay, as if we were taking a trip overseas. We are born in to this world as babies, train ourselves, meet different kinds of people, and go through a variety of experiences so we can build new lives and take on new personalities before returning to the other world. It is for this spiritual training that we come to this world.

It is important that we see our lives in this world from this perspective, but unfortunately, we can't find any textbooks or reference books that clearly state this. As a result, the majority of people today probably believe that such an idea is simply an ancient philosophy or mere superstition. But eventually they'll have to confront the harsh reality that they will all receive fair and accurate assessments of whether their thoughts and deeds in this world were right or wrong according to the values of Truths.

This idea is not unique to Buddhism; ancient Egyptian religion also taught it. Ancient Egyptians believed that after death, they would be judged at the scale of justice to see whether they had been good or bad. Images of the god Thoth recording the results are depicted in ancient Egyptian murals.

Zoroastrianism, the religion of ancient Iran, included a similar teaching. The Zoroastrians believed that after death people must cross a bridge to reach the afterworld. When an evil person tries to cross, the slats of the bridge become as thin as the blades of swords, causing the person to fall, but when a good person crosses, the bridge remains as it is so the person can pass over it safely. This story probably indicates the strictness of the judgment we will face when we cross over to the next world.

These stories have been told around the world. But modern intellectuals often discard them as merely folktales, superstitions, or morality tales that have been created only to encourage people to do good and avoid evil. However, these intellectuals are in fact mistaken; these are true stories of what happens after death.

The truth is not complicated but simple. We should know that the truth is simple and take things as they are taught, straight and simple.

2

Physical Conditions at the Time of Death Influence the Spirit Body for a While

Life in this World Isn't Everything

One of the highly controversial topics that have emerged in recent years relates to organ transplants. From a materialist perspective, it makes sense to see organ transplants as acts of love that can save human lives. In this view, there is nothing wrong with removing healthy organs from virtually dead people and transplanting them to those who need them. But I still have to say that this viewpoint lacks an understanding of the spiritual truth about life and death.

Unfortunately, there are very few people who know what it really means to die. In fact, the vast majority of people have no idea, so the few people who know the truth often have no chance of winning over others in a world where things are settled by majority rule. The positive side of the lack of awareness about the world after death may be that people can focus their efforts on living their best lives in this world. If everybody were highly conscious of the other world, they might be completely enthralled by life after death and neglect life in this world. To prevent this, there are certain aspects of the other world that are hidden from us until we die.

Having said this, we should still not cling to life in this world. It is sufficient if we can do all we can while in this world and live in accordance with the will of God, while achieving a certain level of spiritual awakening in our individual lives. In this regard, we should find contentment in what we can achieve during our limited time in this world.

In addition to the four pains of birth, aging, illness, and death that I mentioned earlier, your life on Earth brings the pain of meeting people you dislike, the pain of parting from your loved ones, the pain of not obtaining what you pursue, and the pain of your physical desires burning furiously through your five senses. These are the eight pains that human beings cannot easily escape in this world. To overcome these pains, it is crucial that we adopt a spiritual outlook on life and perceive this world from the perspective of the real world of the afterlife.

A close study of the teachings of Shakyamuni Buddhism reveals not only that Shakyamuni preached that this world is full of pain and suffering, but also that what he ultimately taught his followers was to abandon their attachments to the physical world. He repeatedly delivered this teaching in a variety of different ways.

To some people, this advice may sound merely like a moral teaching, but the truth is that it is an essential teaching that we need to be able to pass from this world to the next, to move from the three-dimensional material world to the spiritual world of the fourth dimension and beyond. Just as a rocket has to jettison various items before it can escape from the stratosphere, we need to abandon as many worldly values as possible to return to the world of higher dimensions. This is why we need to relinquish our attachments to this world.

☀

An Essential Spiritual Truth to Know
Before an Organ Transplant

Organ transplants seem to be benevolent acts of love, as long as the donor offers the organ with a pure wish to help others and without any worldly attachments. But immediately after death, most people don't yet realize that they are dead. And these people often find it difficult to make a smooth transition to the other world and instead find themselves in great confusion for some time, unable to understand what has happened to them. Even if while they were alive they wished to donate their organs upon their death, it is questionable whether they are able to let go of their attachments to their physical bodies right after their death. Most people cling to their physical body, so when their organs are transplanted into another person, their souls also move into the body of the organ's recipient, spiritually possessing them.

Like the saying, "Give him an inch, and he'll take a mile," organ recipients may end up losing their bodies as compensation for receiving the organs they need. In some cases, the recipient's body rejects the transplanted organ. In many cases where the body accepts the organ, though, the organ recipient undergoes a drastic personality change and becomes a different person altogether.

It's essential that we know the spiritual truth behind this phenomenon. This personality change occurs when the recipient is totally possessed by the spirit of the donor. It is not easy to drive away the donor's spirit, because he will insist that the organ belongs to him. And since his argument is valid in the sense that it was his organ, it is often very difficult to make the donor's spirit leave.

The soul and the body are connected by a silver cord, and when an organ is transplanted, the body of the recipient gets connected to the donor's soul through the silver cord. So it is unavoidable that the recipient takes on a double personality.

The recipient may have no serious issues if the donor of the organ is an angelic person with a good heart, but it's often the case that people receive organs from those who are in a bad condition spiritually. It is said that, in China, they use the organs of the criminals who have been executed for transplant. And if you happen to receive a heart from a gangster who became brain-dead in a shootout, you'll literally have a "hell of a time." You probably don't even want to imagine what kind of person you will end up becoming. So you really don't want to receive an organ from a bad person, because if you do, you'll also inherit the donor's vicious nature.

Spirits of the deceased can possess people living in this world even without organ transplants. Organ transplants make the spirit's attachment all the more strong and let it gain a foothold in the recipient's body. Those who wish to remain in this world often have strong attachments to their physical lives. If such people are given a foothold to a person living in this world, they will remain with the person indefinitely. They become firmly attached to the organ recipient, especially because a part of their consciousness remains with the transplanted organ, making it extremely difficult to dislodge the possessing spirit.

Organ transplantation is a risky procedure spiritually, especially without a good knowledge of the spiritual truth. If you are planning to undergo a transplant operation, I hope that you will do so with an ample understanding of the truth about organ transplants.

※

My Encounters with the Souls of a Deceased Author and a Deceased Actor

What we should all know is that the soul does not part from the body immediately at the moment of death. This is an important truth. Christians misunderstand this, because Christianity teaches that the soul and body are separate and totally unrelated to each other, as in René Descartes's theory of mind-body dualism, but that is not the truth.

In fact, Buddhism offers a much more comprehensive description of the relationship between the soul and the body. The spirit body has a multilayered structure with the core consciousness at its center, and the outer layer is linked to the physical senses. Because of this closely connected relationship, what happens to the physical body exerts considerable influence on the spirit body.

Occasionally, some people return smoothly to the world of higher dimensions immediately after death, but generally it is not so easy to make the transition to the afterworld. Even if you have prior knowledge of the spirit world, you will be scared to go back to it when the time comes, because it will feel like your first death experience.

When the author Tamio Kageyama died, I had a talk with his spirit. As a senior lecturer at Happy Science, he had studied this subject when he was still alive and had sufficient knowledge about what happens after death. But perhaps he didn't expect his death to come so suddenly. It seems that a cigarette butt set fire to his home in the middle of the night, and he lost consciousness due to carbon monoxide poisoning. It was winter and the air was very dry, so the fire spread quickly and he died in the blaze. His spirit came to me after death, but I didn't think he would be able to make a smooth passage to the next world right away. I remember thinking that it would take at least about a month for him to return to the other world. His spirit often appeared in the bathroom and toilet area of my house, so I remember asking him why he kept coming to places that had water. It seems that having died in a fire, he had suffered from terrible thirst, so he appeared in places where there was water. He eventually returned to the other world and currently resides in a higher world of angels-to-be.

A spirit of another senior lecturer at Happy Science, Koji Nanbara, who was a famous Japanese actor, also came to me when he died. He asked me to look after his wife and daughter but said that he had no other physical attachments. I told him he had nothing to worry about, because his wife and daughter were financially secure, and his spirit returned to the other world shortly after that.

☀

The Spirit of a Politician Came to Me the Morning After His Death

Hiroshi Mitsuzuka, a former lower house member who was also a member of our organization, passed away in 2004. He died at night, and at about four o'clock the following morning, I woke up feeling a bit under the weather. I felt that something was not right and wondered what it could be. At that time, I was not aware that Mitsuzuka had died and could not figure out the cause of my feeling of unwellness. At about six forty that morning, I realized that it was the spirit of Mitsuzuka that had come to pay me his respects. I had never met him in person while he was alive, but judging from the way he visited me to say goodbye, it would seem that he had a strong faith in me. He came to me to pass on his dying message.

He was a quiet man and did not speak much. Most spirits are full of self-importance, so when they come to me, I immediately notice their presence. But Mitsuzuka remained still and silent, so it took a while before I realized he was there. After I became aware of his presence, I realized that the discomfort I had felt early morning reflected his condition when he died. He had died in the hospital, and what I experienced were his symptoms at the time of his death.

The soul retains the symptoms of the physical body at the time of death for a period of one or two days after death, and that's why, even when the silver cord is severed, when spirits of the recently deceased come to me, their symptoms at the time of death appear on my body. This does not mean that I became physically ill. It is simply that the symptoms of the spirit that visits me appear in my body. When the spirit body of a person enters into my body, I exhibit the same symptoms that the person had at the time of death, and that's how I can tell how they have died.

※

We Have the Right to Peacefully Set Off for the Afterworld

Saburo Yoshikawa, my father and the Honorary Advisor of Happy Science, died in the summer of 2003, and I took part in his funeral ceremony. When we were preparing for the ceremony, I had a difficult time coping with the many requests his spirit kept making of me. He vetted the list of attendees, telling me who could and could not attend the ceremony. He also gave his opinion of the floral displays and even commented on the treatment of his coffin. He was very opinionated and gave me a hard time.

As I was listening to his requests, I sometimes felt strange chills and wondered why. I often feel a chill when I attend funerals of the people who are scheduled to go to hell, but I knew for sure that this could not be the case for my father, so I found it odd that I felt cold.

I later found out why. His funeral took place in summer, and the coffin had been packed with dry ice to keep the body cool. His soul could feel the coldness of the dry ice while the silver cord still connected the soul to the body. And I could also sense the chill that his soul was feeling. Although I could not make sense of the chills at first, as soon as I heard that the body had been packed in dry ice, I knew exactly why I felt cold.

Our physical body and spirit body overlap with each other immediately after death, so the soul can feel the physical sensations that the person had at the time of death, for example, having an IV drip in one's arm. The soul remains in the same condition as its body for some time after death. If we have our organs removed and transplanted into somebody else in this state, it will most likely hinder our departure to the other world. Most people would not be able to remain calm while their organs are removed after they have just stopped breathing. Those who can instantaneously leave this world and return straight back to the spirit world may have no issues, but the average person is unlikely to have achieved such a high level of awareness.

The souls of the deceased usually linger in the vicinity of their bodies during the funeral service and follow it to the crematorium, listening to what their friends and family are saying. In Japan, it is often said that a soul remains on earth for forty-nine days after death. But in fact, most people do not remain here that long; they travel to the afterworld after about two weeks. During this period, they usually listen to what their families say about them.

Souls usually don't move on to the other world immediately. Even if they've learned about the other world, it is extremely rare for them to return there right after death. Most people worry about the future of their loved ones, so during the two weeks after death, they linger around to eavesdrop on the bereaved.

Some souls are at a loss and act randomly because they have no idea what happens when they die. Whenever I see them, I really wish they had listened to what I have said about the other world, because I have offered a full understanding of the workings of the spirit world.

Although it may not yet be officially recognized as a human right, we all have the right to peacefully die and depart to the afterworld.

A Japanese Politician Asked Me to Deliver a Lecture in Place of a Funeral Service

Those who have recently died often feel frustrated, chagrined, and remorseful for not being able to communicate with people who are still alive; their voices cannot be heard, no matter what they say or how much they try. So when they discover that I am capable of communicating with them, some spirits come to me and ask if I can pass on a message for them.

Normally, the spiritual screen I put around me prevents spirits from approaching me. The spiritual screen surrounding me usually repels spirits, hindering them from coming close to me. Even a spirit of my relative was unable to come to me after death. So a couple of years passed before I became aware that this relative had died. The spirit later told me that it had no idea where I was, because I was completely hidden from view. This is because there is a spiritual screen around me that makes me invisible to spirits.

Although I am usually inaccessible, occasionally, powerful spirits break through my spiritual screen and come to me, as in the cases of the author Tamio Kageyama, the actor Koji Nanbara, and the politician Hiroshi Mitsuzuka. The spirit of the politician Mitsuzuka came to talk to me because he wanted to express his gratitude. He said that he was grateful to the members of Happy Science for all their support. He asked me to look after the future of Japan and talked about a variety of subjects from a politician's standpoint. I told him that there was little I could do to respond to his request that I look after Japan, but he disagreed. He said that Japan would be guided by my words for the next thirty years, so he wanted me to do my best for the country.

To summarize Mitsuzuka's message, he wanted to thank all members of Happy Science. And he came to me because he wanted to listen to my lecture in place of a funeral service. He explained that he really would have liked to have his funeral held at a Happy Science temple in the Happy Science tradition, but he had to hold it at a Buddhist temple because it would be difficult for other politicians and members of the press to attend a Happy Science funeral. He asked me if it would be possible for me to give him one last lecture in place of a funeral service at Happy Science. So I decided to give a lecture about the world after death, so that it will also serve as a Happy Science funeral service for him.

These are some of the examples that show how very real spiritual phenomena are to me. Those around me know this firsthand and realize that spiritual occurrences are the reality. But I find that the more distant people are from me, the less aware they are about spiritual matters. This may be because they are only able to encounter these matters by reading my books or listening to CDs and audio recordings of my lectures. But regardless of the level of their awareness, the truth is that this world is only a temporary abode and is influenced by various factors including the will and thoughts of beings from the invisible world.

I am often struck by the strangeness of my profession. I don't think there is anyone else in Japan or even in the entire world who can give a clearer and more detailed description of the spiritual world. There are numerous psychics in the world, but I doubt that any of them have grasped the truth about the spiritual world, mapped it out, and made assessments about various phenomena as clearly as I have. In this respect, I believe my job carries with it a great responsibility.

I have a clear understanding of all the realms that exist, and I can discern how God will judge various things in this world and the other world from His perspective. Because I have the authority to determine the ideal state we human beings should aim for, I'm able to offer a thorough elucidation of the workings of both this world and the other world. This is one of my greatest strengths and one that I want to continue to cultivate.

3

How to Console the Souls of Your Deceased Family Members and Ancestors

Teach the Truths in a Way the Deceased Can Understand

Consoling the souls of your deceased family members and ancestors is basically a good act, but it has certain risks. Those who didn't believe in the afterworld have nowhere to go when they die, so they are drawn to their offspring who pray for the repose of their souls.

If the souls of your family members or ancestors are suffering in the Hell of Lust or the Hell of Isolation, for example, your earnest prayer of consolation for these souls will appear as a white rope from above coming down to rescue them. They can grip the rope, climb up it, and come out to haunt you. You can save the souls of the deceased if your power is strong enough to guide them to rest in peace, but if you don't have the power to save their souls, you can be drawn into hell. This is why it is essential to have studied the

Truths thoroughly before consoling the souls of the deceased.

If the deceased have no previous knowledge about the world after death, they will not understand my teachings about the afterworld. Just as there are some among the living who do not comprehend the contents of my lectures, some souls of the dead have no idea what I am saying, even if they listen to my lectures. The best they can do is perhaps get a sense that their spiritual vibrations do not resonate with mine. What you need to do in this case is choose a part of my teachings about life after death that will accord with their level of their awareness and explain that part using simple and plain language that they can understand.

It's fine to visit their graves, pay them tribute, and lay flowers on their graves, but when you do, consider whether they made any mistakes in light of the Truths while they were alive, and teach them what you think they need to know to return to heaven. You can speak out loud or speak to them in your heart. Either way, you need to explain them in a simple way that they can understand.

☀

Increase the Power of Your Enlightenment and Receive Support to Save Souls

If, after you have prayed for the souls of the deceased, you feel heavy, unwell, or ill, it probably means that you lack the spiritual power to console their souls. In this case, I recommend that you hold memorial services for these souls at one of the Happy Science temples or centers. It is not easy for individuals to save souls who have fallen to hell.

Death is a major event for human beings. Especially for those who previously had no knowledge of the Truths, the world after death is an insurmountable problem. When they die, they are astonished, thrown into confusion, and panic as if they have been pushed off the top of a tall building. They have no idea what is going on, because they have never seen or heard of the world after death. It takes some time to help and console these souls; it is definitely not an easy task.

We can't save lost souls if we ourselves go astray. We should first concentrate on increasing the power of our enlightenment. In addition, it's safer if we combine our individual strength with the strength of the entire organization when praying for these souls, because without organizational backup, we could be defeated and taken over.

Saving the souls of the deceased is a difficult task. Even if it's a single soul, it takes time and effort to guide it to return to the world of heaven. These souls first need to remember and reflect on all the hardships and experiences they went through while they were alive. They won't be able to set out for the afterworld until they clean and purify their minds through repentance.

When someone you know dies, I recommend that you get together with others who knew the person and together review and reflect on his or her life.

4

Live in a Way that Will Allow You to Face Death with a Smile

In this chapter, I have discussed various topics based on my book *The World of Eternal Life*. Death is a solemn event and the one event that comes to everyone, without exception. When the final moment of your life comes, I hope you will be able to pass away with a smile on your face.

The positive side of advancements in medical science is that they have enabled us to extend longevity, but they also have a negative side: an increasing number of people who suffer at the time of death. We want to die peacefully, because if we die in pain or in anguish, our souls will be similarly afflicted and will be in bad shape spiritually.

It's ideal if we can live happily until one day our silver cord suddenly gets cut off and we set off to the afterworld. Those who have undergone spiritual training at Happy Science should be able to return to heaven within a week of their deaths. Instead of unnecessarily prolonging your stay in this world, I would like to see you ready to return to heaven as soon as your funeral is held.

To make a smooth trip back to heaven shortly after death, we need to abandon any worldly attachments we may have while we are still alive. And to cast off physical bondage, it is essential that we practice self-reflection on a daily basis.

afterword

Perhaps what I've revealed in this book has surprised you. Many readers, no doubt, will find this information hard to believe. But this I can say with certainty: nothing in this book is fiction. Fact is fact, and truth is truth. It is essential that you read this book before your passage to the afterlife. In fact, I believe that this book should be read as early on in life as possible. It holds the knowledge that you need to live in the way that best serves your soul.

If you would like to further deepen your understanding of what I have shared, you can learn more from my other books, including *The World of Eternal Life** and *Finding Faith*†. I, as humanity's teacher, have been born with the

---

* Ryuho Okawa, *Eien no Seimei no Sekai* [The World of Eternal Life] (Tokyo: IRH Press, 2004).

† Ryuho Okawa, *Shinko no Susume* [Finding Faith] (Tokyo: IRH Press, 2005). These books are not currently available in English, but English-speaking readers can learn more about the spirit world in these books: *Spiritual World 101* (New York: IRH Press, 2015), *The Nine Dimensions* (New York: IRH Press, 2012), and *The Laws of Faith* (New York: IRH Press, 2018).

mission to guide this world again, and I have not a shadow of doubt that my teachings of these Truths are destined to reach you.

Ryuho Okawa
Founder and CEO
Happy Science Group

The contents of this book were compiled from the
following lectures by Ryuho Okawa:

Chapter 1:
Life in the World after Death
February 5, 2002

Chapter 2:
Mysteries of the Afterlife Q&A

Q1 The Difference between a Soul and a Spirit: March 5, 1989

Q2 How We Plan for Our Rebirth: May 4, 1987

Q3 What Our Souls Experience during Organ Donation
and Cremation: October 7, 1990

Q4 How to Recognize and Deal with a Negative
Spiritual Influence: April 29, 1992

Q5 The Worlds Where Prominent Poets' Souls Belong:
March 29, 1989

Q6 The Impact of Scientific Progress on the Development
of Our Souls: November 11, 1990

Q7 How Our Souls Evolve through Cycles of Rebirth:
May 28, 1989

Chapter 3:
Modern Developments in the Spirit World
January 28, 2004

Chapter 4:
A Departure for the Afterworld
April 27, 2004

Originally delivered as the second of two lectures for the book
Eien no Seimei no Sekai ("The World of Eternal Life")
[Tokyo: IRH Press, 2004]

About the Author

RYUHO OKAWA is the founder and CEO of a global movement, Happy Science, and international best-selling author with a simple goal: to help people find true happiness and create a better world.

His deep compassion and sense of responsibility for the happiness of each individual has prompted him to publish over 2,300 titles of religious, spiritual, and self-development teachings, covering a broad range of topics including how our thoughts influence reality, the nature of love, and the path to enlightenment. Eastern wisdom that Okawa offers helps us find a new avenue for solutions to the issues we are facing personally and globally now. He also writes on the topics of management and economy, as well as the relationship between religion and politics in the global context. To date, Okawa's books have sold over 100 million copies worldwide and been translated into 30 languages.

Okawa has dedicated himself to improving society and creating a better world. In 1986, Okawa founded Happy Science as a spiritual movement dedicated to bringing greater happiness to humankind by uniting religions and cultures to live in harmony. Happy Science has grown rapidly from its beginnings in Japan to a worldwide organization with over 12 million members in more than 100 countries. Okawa is compassionately committed to the spiritual growth of others. In addition to writing and publishing books, he continues to give lectures around the world.

About Happy Science

Happy Science is a global movement that empowers individuals to find purpose and spiritual happiness and to share that happiness with their families, societies, and the world. With more than twelve million members around the world, Happy Science aims to increase awareness of spiritual truths and expand our capacity for love, compassion, and joy so that together we can create the kind of world we all wish to live in.

Activities at Happy Science are based on the Principles of Happiness (Love, Wisdom, Self-Reflection, and Progress). These principles embrace worldwide philosophies and beliefs, transcending boundaries of culture and religions.

LOVE teaches us to give ourselves freely without expecting anything in return; it encompasses giving, nurturing, and forgiving.

WISDOM leads us to the insights of spiritual truths, and opens us to the true meaning of life and the will of God (the universe, the highest power, Buddha).

SELF-REFLECTION brings a mindful, nonjudgmental lens to our thoughts and actions to help us find our truest selves—the essence of our souls—and deepen our connection to the highest power. It helps us attain a clean and peaceful mind and leads us to the right life path.

PROGRESS emphasizes the positive, dynamic aspects of our spiritual growth—actions we can take to manifest and spread happiness around the world. It's a path that not only expands our soul growth, but also furthers the collective potential of the world we live in.

Programs and Events

The doors of Happy Science are open to all. We offer a variety of programs and events, including self-exploration and self-growth programs, spiritual seminars, meditation and contemplation sessions, study groups, and book events.

Our programs are designed to:

- Deepen your understanding of your purpose and meaning in life
- Improve your relationships and increase your capacity to love unconditionally
- Attain a peace of mind, decrease anxiety and stress, and feel positive
- Gain deeper insights and a broader perspective on the world
- Learn how to overcome life's challenges
  … and much more.

For more information, visit *happyscience-na.org* or *happy-science.org*.

International Seminars

Each year, friends from all over the world join our international seminars, held at our faith centers in Japan. Different programs are offered each year and cover a wide variety of topics, including improving relationships, practicing the Eightfold Path to enlightenment, and loving yourself, to name just a few.

Happy Science Monthly

Our monthly publication covers the latest featured lectures, members' life-changing experiences and other news from members around the world, book reviews, and many other topics. Downloadable PDF files are available at *happyscience-na.org.* Copies and back issues in Portuguese, Chinese, and other languages are available upon request. For more information, contact us via e-mail at *tokyo@happy-science.org.*

Websites

Happy Science
happy-science.org

Happy Science's official website introduces the organization's founder and CEO, Ryuho Okawa, as well as Happy Science teachings, books, lectures, temples, the latest news, and more.

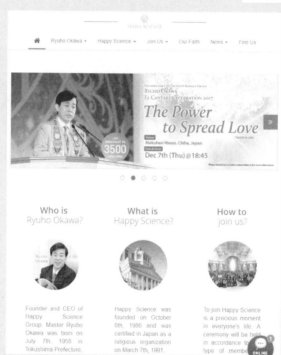

Who is Ryuho Okawa?

Founder and CEO of Happy Science Group, Master Ryuho Okawa was born on July 7th, 1956 in Tokushima Prefecture,

What is Happy Science?

Happy Science was founded on October 6th, 1986 and was certified in Japan as a religious organization on March 7th, 1991.

How to join us?

To join Happy Science is a precious moment in everyone's life. A ceremony will be held in accordance to type of membe

Invitation to Happiness
TV Program Online
invitationtohappiness.org

From August to September 2016, Fox 5 TV aired eight episodes of *Invitation to Happiness*, featuring lectures by Ryuho Okawa, in four states: New York, New Jersey, Connecticut, and Pennsylvania. A second season aired in the summer of 2017 in New York, Atlanta, Los Angeles, San Francisco, and Toronto and received a positive response from viewers. All episodes are available on the website.

Contact Information

Happy Science is a worldwide organization with faith centers around the globe. For a comprehensive list of centers, visit the worldwide directory at *happy-science.org* or *happyscience-na.org*. The following are some of the many Happy Science locations:

United States and Canada

New York
79 Franklin Street New York, NY 10013
Phone: 212-343-7972 Fax: 212-343-7973
Email: ny@happy-science.org
Website: newyork.happyscience-na.org

New Jersey
725 River Rd. #102B
Edgewater, NJ 07020
Phone: 201-313-0127 Fax: 201-313-0120
Email: nj@happy-science.org
Website: newjersey.happyscience-na.org

Florida
5208 8th St. Zephyrhills, FL 33542
Phone: 813-715-0000 Fax: 813-715-0010
Email: florida@happy-science.org
Website: florida.happyscience-na.org

Atlanta
1874 Piedmont Ave. NE Suite 360-C
Atlanta, GA 30324
Phone: 404-892-7770
Email: atlanta@happy-science.org
Website: atlanta.happyscience-na.org

San Francisco
525 Clinton Street,
Redwood City, CA 94062
Phone&Fax: 650-363-2777
Email: sf@happy-science.org
Website: sanfrancisco.happyscience- na.org

Los Angeles
1590 E. Del Mar Blvd. Pasadena, CA 91106
Phone: 626-395-7775 Fax: 626-395-7776
Email: la@happy-science.org
Website: losangeles.happyscience-na.org

Orange County
10231 Slater Ave #204
Fountain Valley, CA 92708
Phone: 714-745-1140
Email: oc@happy-science.org

San Diego
7841 Balboa Ave. Suite #202
San Diego, CA 92111
Phone: 619-381-7615 Fax: 626-395-7776
E-mail: sandiego@happy-science.org
Website: happyscience-la.org

Hawaii
Phone: 808-591-9772
Fax: 808-591-9776
Email: hi@happy-science.org
Website: hawaii.happyscience-na.org

Kauai
4504 Kukui Street, Dragon Building
Suite 207 Kapaa, HI 96746
Phone: 808-822-7007
Fax: 808-822-6007
Email: kauai-hi@happy-science.org
Website: kauai.happyscience-na.org

Toronto
845 The Queensway Etobicoke,
ON M8Z 1N6 Canada
Phone: 1-416-901-3747
Email: toronto@happy-science.org
Website: happy-science.ca

Vancouver
#212-2609 East 49th Avenue,
Vancouver, BC, V5S 1J9 Canada
Phone: 1-604-437-7735
Fax: 1-604-437-7764
Email: vancouver@happy-science.org
Website: happy-science.ca

International

Tokyo
1-6-7 Togoshi, Shinagawa, Tokyo,
142-0041 Japan
Phone: 81-3-6384-5770
Fax: 81-3-6384-5776
Email: tokyo@happy-science.org
Website: happy-science.org

London
3 Margaret Street London,
W1W 8RE United Kingdom
Phone: 44-20-7323-9255
Fax: 44-20-7323-9344
Email: eu@happy-science.org
Website: happyscience-uk.org

Sydney
516 Pacific Hwy, Lane Cove North 2066,
NSW Australia
Phone: 61-2-9411-2877
Fax: 61-2-9411-2822
Email: sydney@happy-science.org

Brazil Headquarters
Rua. Domingos de Morais 1154,
Vila Mariana, Sao Paulo, SP
CEP 04009-002 Brazil
Phone: 55-11-5088-3800
Fax: 55-11-5088-3806
Email: sp@happy-science.org
Website: happyscience.com.br

Jundiai
Rua Congo, 447, Jd. Bonfiglioli,
Jundiai, SP
CEP 13207-340 Brazil
Phone: 55-11-4587-5952
Email: jundiai@happy-science.org

Seoul
74, Sadang-ro 27-gil, Dongjak-gu,
Seoul, Korea
Phone: 82-2-3478-8777
Fax: 82-2- 3478-9777
Email: korea@happy-science.org
Website: happyscience-korea.org

Taipei
No. 89, Lane 155, Dunhua N. Road,
Songshan District,
Taipei City, 105 Taiwan
Phone: 886-2-2719-9377
Fax: 886-2-2719-5570
Email: taiwan@happy-science.org
Website: happyscience-tw.org

Malaysia
No 22A, Block2, Jalil Link,
Jalan Jalil Jaya 2,
Bukit Jalil 57000 Kuala Lumpur, Malaysia
Phone: 60-3-8998-7877
Fax: 60-3-8998-7977
Email: malaysia@happy-science.org
Website: happyscience.org.my

Nepal
Kathmandu Metropolitan City,
Ward No. 15, Ring Road,
Kimdol, Sitapaila Kathmandu, Nepal
Phone: 977-1-427-2931
Email: nepal@happy-science.org

Uganda
Plot 877 Rubaga Road, Kampala
P.O. Box 34130
Kampala, Uganda
Phone: 256-79-3238-002
Email: uganda@happy-science.org
Website: happyscience-uganda.org

About IRH Press USA

IRH Press USA Inc. was founded in 2013 as an affiliated firm of IRH Press Co., Ltd. Based in New York, the press publishes books in various categories including spirituality, religion, and self-improvement and publishes books by Ryuho Okawa, the author of 100 million books sold worldwide. For more information, visit the official author's website at *OkawaBooks.com*.

Also, follow us on

Facebook: OkawaBooks

Twitter: OkawaBooks

Goodreads: RyuhoOkawa

Instagram: OkawaBooks

Pinterest: OkawaBooks

Books by Ryuho Okawa

IRH Press

THE NINE DIMENSIONS

Unveiling the Laws of Eternity

Softcover **168 pages** **$15.95** **ISBN: 978-0-982698-56-3**

This book is a window into the mind of our loving God, who designed this world and the vast, wondrous world of our afterlife as a school with many levels through which our souls learn and grow. When the religions and cultures of the world discover the truth of their common spiritual origin, they will be inspired to accept their differences, come together under faith in God, and build an era of harmony and peaceful progress on Earth.

THE LAWS OF THE SUN

One Source, One Planet, One People

Hardcover **264 pages** **$24.95** **ISBN: 978-1-937673-04-8**

Imagine if you could ask God why he created this world and what spiritual laws he used to shape us—and everything around us. In *The Laws of the Sun*, Okawa outlines these laws of the universe and provides a road map for living one's life with greater purpose and meaning. This powerful book shows the way to realize true happiness —a happiness that continues from this world through the other.

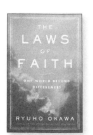

THE LAWS OF FAITH

One World Beyond Differences

Softcover ◦ **208 pages** ◦ **$15.95** ◦ **ISBN: 978-1-942125-34-1**

Ryuho Okawa preaches at the core of a new universal religion from various angles while integrating logical and spiritual viewpoints in mind with current world situations. This book offers us the key to accept diversities beyond differences in ethnicity, religion, race, gender, descent, and so on, harmonize the individuals and nations and create a world filled with peace and prosperity.

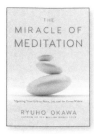

THE MIRACLE OF MEDITATION

Opening Your Life to Peace, Joy, and the Power Within

Softcover ◦ **208 pages** ◦ **$15.95** ◦ **ISBN: 978-1-942125-09-9**

Meditation can open your mind to the self-transformative potential within and connect your soul to the wisdom of heaven—all through the power of belief. This book combines the power of faith and the practice of meditation to help you create inner peace, discover your inner divinity, become your ideal self, and cultivate a purposeful life of altruism and compassion.

THE LAWS OF INVINCIBLE LEADERSHIP
An Empowering Guide for Continuous and
Lasting Success in Business and in Life

THE LAWS OF MISSION
Essential Truths for Spiritual Awakening in a Secular Age

HEALING FROM WITHIN
Life-Changing Keys to Calm, Spiritual, and Healthy Living

THE UNHAPPINESS SYNDROME
28 Habits of Unhappy People (and How to Change Them)

THE LAWS OF SUCCESS
A Spiritual Guide to Turning Your Hopes Into Reality

THINK BIG!
Be Positive and Be Brave to Achieve Your Dreams

THE ESSENCE OF BUDDHA
The Path to Enlightenment

INVITATION TO HAPPINESS
7 Inspirations from Your Inner Angel

MESSAGES FROM HEAVEN
What Jesus, Buddha, Muhammad, and Moses Would Say Today

CHANGE YOUR LIFE, CHANGE THE WORLD
A Spiritual Guide to Living Now

The following books are published by HS Press,
an imprint of IRH Press Co., Ltd.

THE MYSTICAL LAWS
Going Beyond the Dimensional Boundaries

SPIRITUAL WORLD 101
A Guide to a Spiritually Happy Life

For a complete list of books, visit *OkawaBooks.com.*